T

SPACIOUS

HEART

Room for Spiritual Awakening

DONALD CLYMER & SHARON CLYMER LANDIS

Herald Press

Harrisonburg, Virginia
Kitchener, Ontario

Library of Congress Cataloging-in-Publication Data

Clymer, Donald R., 1948-
  The spacious heart : room for spiritual awakening / by Donald R.
Clymer and Sharon Clymer Landis.
    pages cm
  ISBN 978-0-8361-9904-8 (pbk. : alk. paper) 1. Spirituality--
Christianity. 2. Christian life. 3. Spiritual life--Christianity. I.
Title.
  BV4501.3.C58 2014
  248.4--dc23
                                        2014012323

Printed in United States of America
Cover design by Reuben Graham
Cover photo by solarseven / iStock / Thinkstock

To order or request information, please call 1-800-245-7894 in the
U.S. or 1-800-631-6535 in Canada. Or visit www.heraldpress.com.

18 17 16 15 14   10 9 8 7 6 5 4 3 2 1

THE

SPACIOUS

HEART

"Don and Sharon inspire us to enlarge our view of our relationships with God, self, and others. We are drawn to cultivate deeper awareness in listening and looking for the One who lovingly has our best interests at heart."
—**Sheryl Shenk, founder of Blue Ridge Ministries Inc.**

"A book of contrasts—coauthored by a brother and sister who share their personal journeys from cynicism to joy, from the North American culture of dissatisfaction to gratitude, from the mundane to spiritual awakening. This book is rich in personal stories and questions that challenge North American culture, provoke thought, and encourage spiritual growth."
—**April Yamasaki, author of *Sacred Pauses***

"The book inspires deep compassion for the poor along with an equally strong passion for a vital spiritual life. It's rare to see the 'blessed are the poor' in Luke's gospel brought together with the 'blessed are the poor in spirit' in Matthew's in the way the authors do, using memorable stories and insights to illustrate the importance of both dimensions of faith."
—**Harvey Yoder, pastor and professional counselor**

*Dedicated to James and Mary Clymer
in gratitude for their parental example
of allowing life and faith to expand their hearts.*

TABLE OF CONTENTS

Foreword

I was eager to read this book by the brother and sister team of Donald R. Clymer and Sharon Clymer Landis since both are Mennonite, and I was not disappointed in *The Spacious Heart: Room for Spiritual Awakening*. In fact, several of the traits that are usually associated with Mennonites make this one of the best books on spiritual disciplines that I have ever read.

The first trait one notices is this book's emphasis on justice. Don has experience working with the intensely poor as a mission worker in Latin America, and the first two chapters highlight fairness as a focus for spiritual growth and life. Among Christian denominations this is one domain in which the Mennonites excel, and all of us who follow Jesus have much to learn from them.

Another unique dimension is the accent on *Gelassenheit* in chapter 8. Jesus, of course, is the best model of this characteristic, which is a willingness to suffer for the sake of God. It can also be described as a virtue of peace and calmness of mind. A very important quality of the spirituality of Christians for the sake of this hectic, harried civilization, *Gelsassenheit* is an attribute of serenity and tranquility in the face of strain and tension.

Similarly, this book calls for mercy instead of *Schadenfreude*, or delight at another person's affliction (chapter 10). In a society of jealousy and vindictiveness against other people, Christians are needed to be an alternative community that models compassion and goodness and empathy.

There are many other typical Mennonite distinctions that I would like to point out, but it is better if you read Don's and Sharon's writing instead of mine, so I will close by mentioning an aspect of their collection's style that especially suits this volume's subject. Because each chapter displays a negative type of drivenness, which plagues our culture's citizens, the Clymer brother and sister team do not explain spiritual practices by dogmatic exposition. Instead, they draw us into various skills and habits by telling us stories about them.

Their narratives lovingly invite us to imitate the processes and procedures exhibited for the sake of our own hearts, leading us to become more spacious and open for all that God wants to do in and with us.

My spiritual life and practices were immensely strengthened by pondering this book. I pray the same for you!

Marva J. Dawn
Theologian, Author, Speaker
Vancouver, Washington

Acknowledgements

We offer gratitude to our editor at Herald Press, Melodie Davis, for her insight, enthusiasm, patience, and support; Avery Peters, copyeditor, for her critical eye and keen editorial suggestions; Amy Gingerich, editorial director, and Reuben Graham, designer, for the catchy cover design; Tyler Tully for the marketing blurb; and Harvey Yoder for suggesting our eventual title, *The Spacious Heart*.

I (Sharon) also offer much gratitude to my brother Don, for his gentle persuasion to coauthor this book and his ongoing encouragement and humor; my husband, Jay, a quiet gem of a man who not only graciously allowed me to write about him, but also learned to cook solo and care for our grandchildren while I wrote; my precious family for their constant support, especially daughter Stephanie for the photo shoot and resulting author photo; my first writing teacher, Brenda Witmer, for her kind instruction in silencing my inner critic; the small nurturing church where I grew up; the amazing teachers and community of Kairos: School of Spiritual Formation; and every friend and companion who shared their life and spiritual journey with me. Each one has a special place in my heart.

ॐ

I (Don) would like to acknowledge with gratitude my sister Sharon for following through on her life's dream of being published, in spite of learning of the idea during an intense recovery period from a bout with cancer. I am also grateful to innumerable colleagues who had to bear with me as I tested my new ideas on them, especially Paul Souder and Omar Eby, who offered useful advice and critique, and to my three cross-cultural groups from Eastern Mennonite University (2007, 2010, and 2012), who provided endless amounts of material for stories. I'd like to thank Kelly Brewer Dean for a photo shoot that provided me with a professional portrait at no cost. Finally, I want to acknowledge my wife, Esther, who has been a consistent companion through many of the faith struggles that made me a cynical, stonehearted person. Her steadfastness and support helped me move toward a more spacious heart.

Introduction

Several colleagues and I (Don) were sitting around a table at a Christian university. One of my colleagues went on and on about how modest his salary was, and the sacrifice he was making to teach at this university. My mind pictured his lovely country home and large late-model SUV, and I wondered what else he needed. My mind also pictured my friend Ricardo from the rural village in Mexico where I had worked and how he had to scrimp and save just to put decent food on the table.

ঽ৯

I was waiting in line for lunch in the cafeteria of a Christian college. The student in front of me asked a student who was leaving, "What's for lunch today?" The departing student, with a look of disgust on her face, snarled, "the same old stuff."

I was at the college for a series of meetings about my work with a mission agency in a rural village in Mexico. I wanted to grab the student and tell her, "I know hundreds of families in our village who would be delighted to eat that."

જ⁀

A new acquaintance of mine and I were discussing my view of Jesus' ministry. I said I preferred the description "radical" to "conservative" or "liberal." I was at a language school with other missionaries preparing for service in Latin America. Another man who overheard our conversation came up to me and said, "A radical is a liberal is a Communist." That sort of ended our fine conversation.

જ⁀

I stood in front of the shelves of breakfast cereal boxes in a supermarket. There were hundreds to choose from. Where my family lived in rural Mexico, our supermarket carried six different cereals: two brands of cornflakes, two brands of bran cereal, one brand of sugar-coated cornflakes, and Wheaties.

I was dumbfounded. I had no idea where to begin in my search for a breakfast cereal. Frustrated, I chose the cornflakes.

જ⁀

A woman at a nearby table was busily looking at her hands on her lap while I was at an all-day church conference. Her fingers kept dancing over the face of the little instrument she carried in her hand. Occasionally she would look up to listen to the speaker, but she soon returned to her tapping. This went on with a few pauses throughout the day. I wondered what was so important in her life that she couldn't be present to the other people in the room.

ॐ

As portrayed in these stories, our culture is overwhelmed. We have too many choices—too many options to fill our time that can leave us stressed out, fearful, lonely, and ungrateful. Our culture could use fresh approaches to life and leisure and new ways of experiencing God to help us face these challenges. We could all benefit by becoming more mellow of heart, a heart that is open and allows more room for God.

Introduction to the Authors
Sharon and Don are brother and sister, and they grew up in a large family of eleven siblings. Having so many siblings resulted in what appeared to be two different families. Don was in the first half of the family, Sharon in the second. They barely knew each other growing up. Don is male and Sharon is female, and this gives them varying interpretations of what it means to belong to this huge clan. Don was extroverted and easily engaged others while Sharon was shy.

Somehow in midlife, they both became aware of something they had in common: a mystical bent to life. Don discovered his while dealing with the grinding oppression he encountered in Latin America as a mission worker. Sharon didn't have to discover hers; it was always present. She just needed tools to name what she was experiencing. Both received training as spiritual directors without the other knowing it. What fun it was to suddenly discover a new sister and a new brother! Thus began their journey in putting together this book.

Introduction to Don
I first came across the concept of mellowness of heart as an important part of spirituality while reading chapter 3 of Ronald Rolheiser's seminal work *The Holy Longing*.[1] He called "mellowness of heart" one of the "nonnegotiable

essentials" of Christian spirituality along with private prayer
and morality, social justice, and participation in a community
of faith.[2] Three of the essentials made sense to me, and at
least two of them seem to be standard expectation in most
Christian expressions of faith. The one on social justice is
less often included in conservative evangelical expressions
of Christian spirituality. On the other hand, the Mennonite/
Anabaptist tradition both Sharon and I are a part of has historically recognized social justice as part of the message of
Jesus. I have been blessed through much personal experience
working with the very poor in Central America and Mexico,
so Rolheiser's inclusion of social justice as part of a healthy
spirituality was no surprise.

Mellowness of heart, however, jumped out at me as being quite odd. In spite of our training in spiritual formation,
nowhere had either my sister or I encountered this concept.
There is little if any reference to such an idea in spiritual
formation literature. There is no reference to it in any theological works of which we are aware. In fact, the word *mellowness* cannot even be found in the Bible. First Peter 3:8
mentions a "tender heart" (NRSV) as one in a list of qualities
for Christians to demonstrate: "Finally, all of you, have unity
of spirit, sympathy, love for one another, a tender heart, and
a humble mind." This probably comes as close to Rolheiser's
idea as any. So we are left with the question, How could it
possibly be a "nonnegotiable essential" of Christian spirituality? Could it be as important a concept as the other three?

Perhaps the fact that the idea was so foreign to me and
because of my general curiosity about spiritual formation,
I began to let the idea soak in, and I started to read the
Scripture in a totally different way. At first blush, the word
mellowness is so counter to the cultural milieu within which
both my sister and I were nurtured that we struggled to understand Rolheiser's idea. First, there is the Protestant work
ethic so prevalent in the general culture of the United States.
To work hard to get ahead and stay ahead causes more stress
than mellowness. Then add the Reformed tradition's concept

of total depravity (see our glossary at the back of the book for theological or other terms related to spirituality that may not be familiar to you) which has seeped consciously or unconsciously into the psyche of those from my Mennonite upbringing through revival and renewal movements of the '50s and '70s if not before. Unfortunately, combating the worminess of our God-given nature is the cause of much more stress and anxiety, producing anything but mellowness.

Finally, the emphasis of my faith tradition on discipleship—a strict following of the teachings of Jesus in the Sermon on the Mount—leads to an emphasis on "perfectionism," to which no one can ever measure up. Stress, anxiety, and more stress. I found plenty of places in our spiritual heritage as well as practice where mellowness was needed—indeed, mellowness of heart. This is a fairly universal need. As spiritual directors my sister and I have both dealt with spiritually wounded people from many traditions as well as seekers from no tradition at all. Most of these people could use a more balanced spirituality, especially one that includes the mellowness of heart identified by Rolheiser.

After much reflection on this theme, and after testing several concepts with work groups and in retreats, we came to the conclusion that the concept of mellowness of heart needed further development. Hence, we wrote this book.

Mellowness involves a spacious, or open, heart. It can be a tender heart—a heart that is receptive to growing understandings of God and spirituality. However we describe it, a person with such a heart is one who is more laid back, more willing to experience God's presence in all aspects of life.

Introduction to Sharon

I believe God's love is an experience, not just a comforting theology. It is my hope that the stories shared in the story sections of our book will encourage you to notice, validate, and cherish the gentle way God interacts with you. I offer many stories in

this book: my own and those of friends and folks who come to me for spiritual direction. Even when they've given me permission, I've changed their names and circumstances as their stories really belong to them, and I treat all stories as sacred. I am grateful for their willingness to share the joy and difficulty that is prayer and spiritual growth. May you also seek people and places of safety and begin sharing your God encounters so humanity may collectively experience the richness, depth, abundant love, creativity, and playfulness of God.

EXPERIENCING GOD: GOD AS A FOUNTAIN OF LIGHT, LOVE, ENERGY (SHARON)

Humanity is awash in God experiences. Like the absurdity of a fish seeking the sea, we seek God and often forget we aren't separated from God. Experiences of God simply are, whether or not we are aware. We sing these lyrics to the song "Prayer for Peace," "Christ before us, Christ behind us, Christ under our feet. Christ within us, Christ over us, let all around us be Christ," while remaining blind to God, and afraid. Along with an open heart and eyes to see, we need practice sharing our stories of God. We struggle to find words for our experiences; we fear the cynicism or doubt from others. Yet, I believe stories of God are what sustain and inspire us. Each story reveals a different face of God; when people or groups of people remain silent about their God stories, my view is limited. When stories are shared our collective vision of God is enriched and expanded.

In Romans 8:38-39, Paul says nothing can separate us from the love of God. Not life or death, not angels or demons, not the present or the future, not height or depth. Nothing can separate us from the love of God, but sometimes the human heart feels unworthy and unable to receive the fullness of God's love. It might be easier to open our heart's door to receive salvation than to receive the lavishness of God's love.

Receiving God's love takes faith that is more heart than mind, more mystery than logic or reason, and thus the God experiences that deeply move us are difficult to put into words. Religious language can be a real deterrent to people sharing or even wanting God experiences, so I'm learning to use words that are more real for me and more hopeful for others. God becomes Divine Love or Truth, Beauty, Goodness, Life. The Holy Spirit is the Spirit of Love. Christ for me means Love, and Christ is the very energy that enlivens the whole universe with the energies of love, compassion, creation, birth, suffering, death, regrowth, and resurrection.

Years ago, when I started a more intentional spiritual journey, I began going to a spiritual director. At first, I feared what I would be asked to do or what I might experience. During one session my director asked me how I was experiencing God. After searching for words, I finally told her God felt like a fountain of light, love, and energy flowing over my body and through my soul. I also told her God allows me to have a faucet to control the flow.

"Why do you need to control the flow?"

"I don't know . . . maybe I'd be knocked flat . . . maybe I'd have too much energy . . . or maybe I'm still a little afraid of it."

"Tell me more about your fear," she said.

"I'm afraid if I sit under the full flow, I'll become really different, perhaps too spiritual, and then I won't relate well to people."

She thought for a moment, and then said, "You've named this fear so you can hold it up and look at it. I invite you to examine it in the presence of God." She closed her eyes; I assumed she was inviting me to pray.

I felt anxious and a bit deserted. I didn't want to face God with nothing but my fear. I wished my director would pray with me or for me, but I closed my eyes and quieted myself.

I thought how easy it was to journal my deep thoughts or think my prayers, or allow love to flow from my heart to God. I thought how scary it was to pray with transparency, inviting Christ to sit with me and examine things I didn't understand and feared. Being a visual person, I wondered what my fear might look like, so I asked God for an image.

Instantly, the image of the moon I saw the night before came to mind. The moon was full and vibrant, surrounded by a gentle, golden halo of light. I remembered staring at the moon, sensing some insight forming within me, but I was content to simply drink in the beauty and not force awareness. The memory of the moon felt sacred, as if it were a gift from God.

Suddenly, I felt immersed in a deep, warm, refreshing current. My skin tingled as insight dawned. In the moon, God had given me a vision of love instead of an image of my fear. The moon represented me, and the gentle halo around the moon represented God: God all around me, softly supporting me, sustaining me, inspiring me, holding me, loving me. In my vision, the moon was shining, not God. Tears welled up in my eyes as I realized Holy God was coming to me, purposely and lovingly dimmed, so I would not be overwhelmed.

My fears vanished. This God I can trust and welcome into my deepest self without fear. I can move under the Divine Flow, without the need for control, because God will never overwhelm me or ask me to be anything other than what I was created to be. I can shine, fully illuminated with God's love, without fearing I'll lose my grip on reality. I sat quietly, contemplating God's tenderness, marveling how God must come to each seeker in the exact way they need to receive healing and love.

My director asked me what I was experiencing and I told her.

"So, how does it feel to shine?" she asked, a wide smile on her face.

I had no words, only a wide smile of my own. For the rest of the session we sat in silence, our faces beaming and our souls basking in the presence of Divine Love.

CHAPTER 1

Basking in the Presence of Divine Love

THE MAKING OF A CYNIC (SHARON)

A young girl sat on the porch rubbing the ears of a beautiful gray tabby cat. There was nothing special about the cat—a thousand cats are gray tabbies—unless you consider that this particular tabby was the girl's best friend. Saved from starvation with some of the girl's own dinners, gray cat showed gratefulness by rubbing his cheek against her shoulder. His fat, sleek, grown-up belly was satisfied with bits of cat food bought secretly though hoarded babysitting money. Affection passed easily between girl and cat. Each afternoon contained a happy reunion as the girl leaped off the school bus and greeted this purring, leg-rubbing gray cat.

Weekends were bliss. Every spare moment between seemingly endless chores, girl and cat sat together in the sunshine of the porch, or out in the grass, or on a tree limb. The girl told the cat everything in her heart and in return the cat brought the best of his kills to share with her: a rabbit outside the door, a half-chewed rat by the porch rug. They took care of each other, and the girl understood this cat's language of love even when saddened by the dead animal offerings.

One beautiful sunny Saturday morning, the girl happily got out of bed without having to be called. Something awakened her early. Light-hearted and full of anticipation, she dressed quickly, hoping to savor extra time with Gray before breakfast and chores. She opened the porch door and saw no sign of her hungry cat. She looked everywhere. Soon visions of Gray run over by a car or other dreadful worries filled her mind. *Ah, I'm early,* she thought and comforted herself, *Gray is still out hunting.* She ate breakfast. She read a book and then as her siblings got up and the day's activities began, the girl filled the cat food dish, shook it, making the kibble rattle louder and called, "Here kitty, kitty, kitty." Gray never missed breakfast. He never missed the sound of the bag crackling or the kibble clattering into the bowl. The girl's calls filled the porch, then the yard, then slowly and agonizingly, they repeated down the roads near her house.

Hours later she entered the kitchen, heart in eyes, and asked Mom if she saw Gray this morning. Mom hesitated, turning her back, then swiftly, as if to negate the rawness of everything presenting this awful morning, she explained.

"Dad took him to the auction. Wake up, girl! You had to know what happened to all your cats, all these years, when they reached a certain weight! You couldn't be that naive."

But, the girl was naive. A complete idealist, this child's heart was as open and wide as the sky above. In her eleven years she had tried to harden, wise up, become cynical and tough. This particular morning, as realization dawned and grief leaned toward rage, her heart succeeded in wrapping itself in an extra hard layer of distrust and stoic resolve.

She remembered other Saturday mornings and missing cats. Saturday was "small animal market" day at the local auction; how could she have not put two and two together? Her mind closed down right after her heart walled itself up. If she imagined her beloved pets, the ones she rescued and saved, now caged as lab animals, tortured, experimented on, powerless, well, she wouldn't have survived her guilt. She wasn't ready to own that she hadn't saved them at all, but delivered them, fat and healthy, into her worst nightmare.

Many of our childhood experiences are wounding. Though the young girl in this story is me, the child is symbolic of every child. This is a universal story: the struggle to understand our culture, and the struggle to grow up. We all begin innocent and openhearted, loving, and possibly remembering perfect unity with the Loving Consciousness that breathed us into being. Life eventually hurts us and we wrap ourselves in layers of armor. If we get hurt or our dreams are dashed often enough we can become jaded, skeptical, and cynical. The transformation of cynicism into joy becomes part of our healing, part of our faith journey.

I have told you this so that my joy may be in you and that your joy may be complete. —John 15:11

.... ## FROM CLOWN TO CYNIC (DON)

When I was in high school, I was considered the class clown. "Wit wins him many friends," was inscribed under my picture in our yearbook. Unfortunately this relentless jocularity also got me into trouble. I was called to the principal's office of the private Mennonite high school that I attended because he had heard too many complaints that I never took anything seriously. As a class officer, I was to represent staid sensibility and docile decorum. Instead, I was heard laughing loudly in the halls, cutting it up with my friends, and generally having a good time.

This all changed when I went to Honduras, Central America, to work with Mennonite Voluntary Service, an organization of the Mennonite Church. I was there as a conscientious objector (CO) during the Vietnam War, fulfilling a two-year obligation to the U.S. government. To be sure, the change didn't happen overnight, but it evolved slowly over the next several years. At nineteen years of age, I was thrust out of my naive and isolated world in rural Pennsylvania into the world of intercultural relationships and the poverty of a developing world. I had no idea how profoundly this experience would affect me. What affected me was the grinding poverty I saw. I couldn't explain the disparity between my lifestyle—lower middle class at best in my home country— and the way people were doomed to live in Honduras, especially in the more rural areas. Illiteracy and malnutrition were endemic, and what really surprised me was discovering, through Honduran friends, the role that my own nation had played in keeping the majority of the people living in such meager conditions.

Telling Their Story Made Me Angry

One of those Honduran friends told me when I left, "Don't ever forget what you saw and learned while you were here. Tell our story to everyone you meet." So that's what I set out to do. I became a Spanish teacher and used every opportunity to tell their story of poverty, oppression, and empire in my classes. I told their story in church. What I didn't realize until many years later that slowly I became more and more angry as I retold their story.

While my contemporaries in the United States continued to explain away Jesus' numerous teachings on the dangers of wealth with the statement, "It's your attitude toward money that matters, not the actual amount of wealth you have," my brothers and sisters in Honduras and many other Latin American countries continued to slip further and further into the depths of poverty. And while my contemporaries in the United States built ever larger homes to live in and drove ever more expensive vehicles, my friends in Latin America were faced with new threats to whatever little economic progress they had made through neoliberal economic policies that overwhelmingly favored the bankers and business interests of the overdeveloped world.

What I failed to see in my outrage was that many of those whom I knew that were entrapped in the worst poverty, although poor in material things, were very rich in spirit. They were more dependent on God, and they saw God in even the simplest of things. And above all, as we will see in the chapter on gratitude, they took nothing for granted and were thankful for every small thing that came their way. Along with being dependent on God, they were dependent on each other for their mere survival.

A Frustrated Idealist

I excused my inner rage as righteous indignation, similar to the prophetic tradition of the Hebrew Bible, but it was slowly eating away at my soul. My entering the world of academia didn't help very much. At first I thought I was gaining an intellectual framework on which to hang my wrath through studying progressive, even Marxist, social systems, liberation theology, and depth psychology. Unfortunately, the higher that you climb the scholastic ladder, the more expert you become at deconstructing; tearing everything down while too frequently failing to build a new foundation from the ruins of your former belief system. You learn to criticize everything. The combination of my anger and my education made me the ultimate cynic. The happy-go-lucky, never-take-anything-seriously youth had died. In his stead there appeared a bitter, cynical, critical man headed for a crisis. If I wasn't miserable with myself, I made everyone around me miserable.

Cynicism sucks the joy out of one's character. It also takes away hope. Cynicism, according to David Mazella in his book *The Making of Modern Cynicism*, is "a future without hope, without meaningful change."[1] He described me perfectly in quoting this adage: "underneath every cynic lies a disappointed idealist."[2] How I had hoped that things would improve for my friends in Latin America and that true political and economic reforms would take place. The promise of new social movements was crushed by brutal repression in the form of some of the cruelest dictatorships known to humankind; business-inclined U.S. politicians propped up most of these dictatorships. The promise of a new theology in which the poor were exalted "on earth" as they were "in heaven" was crushed by waves of "prosperity gospel" and "pie-in-the-sky-by-and-by" eschatology washing over the growing evangelical religious scene.

Both theological waves, the prosperity gospel and the pie-in-the-sky eschatology, unwittingly propped up the economic and political policies of the empire to the North. True prophetic social justice as taught by the Hebrew prophets and Jesus himself was seen as an unbiblical theory of radicals. These were the roots of my anger and cynicism. These were the roots of my impending crisis.

A Spiritual Crisis

Even though at the time I couldn't have identified myself as either angry or cynical, I thought I could cure my life's frustration by returning to Latin America and working directly with the issues of poverty and oppression. I spent three more years with Mennonite Central Committee (MCC) in Mexico. While there, I was in a meeting with a group of young Mexican Mennonite church leaders. We were sharing our life stories with each other. When it was my turn, I explained my frustrations by calling them my "mid-life crisis" and by using other psychological terms. A young woman looked me in the eyes and said, "It sounds to me like you are having a spiritual crisis, brother."

It would have hurt less had she slapped me across my face. In one sentence she had stripped my mask off and exposed my hypocrisy to the world. Who was I to be a representative of the gospel on the "mission field" when I was in the midst of a spiritual crisis? That statement was pivotal in making me look for a deeper spirituality, for a mellower heart, for a way to melt my icy cynicism and assuage my anger. It did not happen overnight and I continue on the journey. The happy-go-lucky personality has returned without the person who never takes anything seriously. The "spiritual crisis" forced me learn how to reflect deeply. It forced me to turn inward—to find my soul and the pre-birth, God-given joy residing there.

Overcoming Angry Cynicism

One does not have to travel abroad and have an encounter with the issues I'd faced in order to become cynical. The same can happen to people who have been involved in a personal crisis such as the catastrophic death of a loved one, the break-up of a significant relationship, a life-threatening illness or disability, or the loss of a job. Some of these events blindside the person involved, while other crises develop over a long period of time. In either case, cynicism becomes the coping device used to deal with the overwhelming sense of living a "future without hope." To work at healing this cynicism, one needs to open one's heart. One does this by developing the joy that Jesus talks about in John 15:11: "I have told you [his disciples] this so that my joy may be in you and that your joy may be complete." What did he tell his disciples? That God loves them and that they should remain in that love in order to make their joy complete—in order to develop a heart with room for a spiritual awakening.

Finding Inner Joy and a More Spacious Heart

I stated earlier that my cynicism forced me to turn inward. Turning inward helped me discover the essence of who I am, the God-likeness found in my soul—the true image of God in which I was created. There I found the joy of being beloved of God. Many saints over the ages have spoken about one's intimacy with God before being born. "Inside each of us, be-yond what we can name, we have a dark memory of having once been touched and caressed by hands far gentler than our own," writes Ronald Rolheiser. "That caress has left a permanent mark, the imprint of love so tender and good that its memory becomes a memory through which we see everything else."[3]

As Rolheiser points out, after birth, one is plagued by a vague memory of that intimacy, papered over by a mortal body and layers of socialization. Restlessness results. A restlessness that is really a "holy longing," a yearning to return to the intimacy that one once had with God before birth. St. Augustine expresses it best in his *Confessions*: "You have made us for yourself, O Lord, and our heart is restless until it rests in you."

Turning inward to the soul, or to the unconscious, as depth psychiatrists like Carl Jung call it, is not all light and joy. In fact, one needs to pass though many layers of socialization and voices from our families and culture to arrive at the core of our being, our soul. These layers contain the egocentric and ethnocentric pride that causes us to turn from our essential goodness and to sin.

Ninth-century Celtic philosopher John Scotus Erigena believed that "when we look within ourselves, and within all that exists, we will find darkness and evil but, deeper still the goodness of God."[4] Our inward journey can be long and arduous, but eventually we discover the reason for our creation, for our existence. We subdue our restless hearts, our holy longing, and find our rest in God. We return to the intimacy we remember from before our birth. We bask in God's love for us. Our joy is complete.

Joy through Active Imagination

How is this done? There are many ways to turn inward. Since most of this chapter has been about my own personal journey, I will continue on that path by sharing what has been most helpful for me. Among the main thresholds for entering my unconscious that I found useful are active imagination, meditative walks, and music.

Active imagination is a technique that is useful for turning inward.[5] Growing up, my parents discouraged my active imagination. They considered it to be evil. Yet the relationship between image and imagination should be clear. We are made in the image of God; God imagined us and created us. Imagination and creation are cousins. When we use our imaginations, not only are we using our God image-ness, but we are also creating.

I envision myself sitting on a log on the shore of an alpine lake. There is such a lake near my spouse's home in Switzerland. The scenery is gorgeous. I invite characters that have appeared from my unconscious, mostly through dreams, to sit with me and have a conversation. We talk about why they have visited me in my dream and I challenge them or ask them for forgiveness. Sometimes I invite Jesus to join me. We talk about issues that I am dealing with in my conscious life. I often ask Jesus for forgiveness. There are times when characters I did not invite show up. Sometimes we argue, sometimes we laugh together. I always leave these scenes feeling more complete, more filled with gratitude and joy.

Joy through Meditative Walks

Meditative walks are another excellent way to turn inward. Over the years I have used a number of techniques to help the process. Some days I take a verse of Scripture along with me on my walk and repeat it over and over. It doesn't have to be a long portion of Scripture. A few meaningful phrases are enough. For example, "The Lord is my shepherd, I shall not want" from the twenty-third Psalm, or "Thy will be done on earth as in heaven," from the Lord's Prayer. The rhythm of one's breathing, the repetition of the biblical phrases along with the steady beat of one's feet help to bring one into the presence of God.

Sometimes I use a song instead of a Bible verse. A hymn by George Beverly Shea runs through my mind: "I love thy presence Lord, the place of secret prayer. My soul communes with thee, and gone is earthly care. I love thy presence Lord

to me thou art made real, as when on Galilean hills thy loving touch didst heal." Or I listen to a version of it on my iPod
while I walk. Again, the combination of breathing, repeating,
and walking produces the elements necessary to feel the presence of God right with me.

One of my favorite methods is repeating the Jesus Prayer
over and over again in rhythm with my walking and breathing, "Lord Jesus Christ, son of God, have mercy on me, a
sinner." Many Christian religious practitioners have used this
prayer over the centuries as a way to bring them into the
presence of God, to work at praying ceaselessly. Once while
in the midst of this prayer, I saw a huge cloud formation on
the horizon. It opened up, and two loving arms reached down
and embraced me. I have returned in my active imagination
many times to rest in this image of forgiveness, providence,
and comfort that was brought on by this prayer. This rest
has also helped remind me that God loves me and that I can
remain in that love—that in that love my joy is complete and
my heart becomes more seasoned.

Joy through Music

Breath, rhythm, and movement somehow put one in touch
with the broader rhythms of the universe and with the "heartbeat of God." The ancient Celts would intone their time-hon-
ored prayers, passed on by oral tradition from generation to
generation, by the sea. This was "so their voices might join
the 'voicing of the waves' and their praises the 'praises of
the ceaseless seas.'"[6] Music contains all these elements. So to
music I turn.

Music has always been a very important part of my life.
As I think about turning my cynicism into joy, I can't help
but refer to music. During my darkest, most cynical days,
music lifted my spirits. This is fairly universal. "Whenever I
feel depressed I grab my guitar," stated a student in a discussion about music in one of my classes. "I sing and play until
my spirit is lifted and my mood is changed." Another student
added, "sometimes I like to sing, and sometimes I just like to
listen. Either way, music moves me."

Many times God touched my soul through music whether I wanted it or not. Like repeatedly calling Samuel, God kept nudging me to recognize my heartfelt soul-stirrings, but I kept pushing God aside. On one occasion I was driving across the country alone listening to a classical piece of choral music. In spite of my stoic, cynical self, I was so moved by emotion that I had to pull to the side of the road. I wept uncontrollably for several minutes. My whole body shook. My soul was cleansed. My tears were joyful.

Whether I realized it or not, these tears were reminding me of an earlier intimacy with God that my experiences and socialization had made me abandon. Perhaps, unbeknownst to me, I was "joining the voice of the whole universe in giving praise to God."[7] This experience was a signpost for me to return to from time to time during my most bitter and cynical days. This experience was one of the stronger nudges from God that I received through music. I received many more during my darkest times.

Don McCormick, in his book *Companions: Christ-Centered Prayer*, claims that "Singing [music] can be a deeply passionate form of prayer."[8] I believe that what I called nudges from God through music were such passionate prayers bubbling up from my unconscious that they needed to be expressed. Since my cynicism kept me from voicing those deepest longings of my heart in a more traditional prayer form, God used what would get my attention. Since my happier self has returned, I continually return to the beauty of music as a passionate form of prayer to refresh my joy. This tempers any tendency to return to my past cynicism.

Recently three different people told me that I am always smiling. What a contrast to the scowl I carried around in my cynical, angry days. Using active imagination, meditative walks, and music has helped me overcome my cynicism. The smile others noticed truly represents the progress I have made toward making my joy complete and developing a mellow heart.

❧

.... **EXPERIENCING GOD: A DEEPLY CARING MOTHER (SHARON)**
The next story takes place decades after my cat story and
involves another interaction between Mom and me. First, I
want to mention how the cat story shaped my growing up
years. After that day, I began closing up emotionally by trying to hide my sensitivity and hardening my heart towards
vulnerability in any relationship. I thought this was the way
of maturity and formed strong but false beliefs about love.

Many do likewise. In the first half of life we guard our
wounds, defend or inflate our sense of self, convincing ourselves our perceptions and judgments are right. The next half
involves peeling off those layers and gaining some distance
from our hurts and perceptions in order to rediscover and
uncover our truest self, and while doing so we surprisingly
find a deeper sense of God. Neither stage is age related. In
their twenties, some people begin the peeling process; mid-
life transitions catapult others into doing so. Some are too
wounded to ever start, and some do so right before death.
I share my cat story as part of my own peeling process, and
not to blame my parents or myself for any misconceptions
or wrongdoing. The first story sets the stage for the second
story. Both stories show how this peeling process brings a
deeper connection to ourselves, to God, and thus we move
from cynicism to joy.

Now, I understand my father was doing exactly what
my cat did in bringing me offerings of wild-caught food. My
dad was simply taking care of his family. A pragmatic man,
he sold what he could sell to provide. He did not have the
luxury to get to know each of his children, especially not the
quiet ones that didn't demand attention. Our culture did not
encourage reflection on life and personal discernment about
choices and actions. I do not make excuses for him, and neither do I blame him. We all do the best we can with what we
know about ourselves and others.

However, that hurtful "cat" day of discovery added fuel to the fires of my doubt that God is kind and life is safe. It burned away my natural idealism and dulled any willingness toward full emotional expression. Angry and ashamed of my deep connection with animals, I tried not to care so much. Deeply felt emotions weren't acceptable to me; denial became my coming-of-age story. Disowning or hiding in self-protection, hardening to fit in, to ease pressure, to please, or to belong has consequences. I became guarded, skeptical, closed to a deepening relationship with myself, hindering my ability to relate to God and others. Life felt shallow. It was good at times, but overall lacking in depth, authenticity, and meaning.

After years harboring anger at my dad and God, I was able to let it go. Underneath the anger, I found another wound that needed attention: a sense of emotional abandonment from Mom. Again, after allowing myself to feel, heal, and release, I came to realize Mom was simply a product of the wider cultural mistrust of emotion. Our culture lauded strength, hard work, obedience, analytical thought, independence, and control of one's mental and emotional self. While laughing and singing were acceptable, those emotions we judged as "powerful" or "negative" were not. Thus, my sweet, sensitive mother could not be present to me in ways she was unable to be present to herself.

Children tend to be better at impersonating parents than doing what they are told to do. Mom and I are no exception. We both absorbed our cultural distrust of emotions, distrust of intuitive or gentle approaches to spirituality, and stifled ourselves. Passivity in women was valued in Mom's day, but for me it paved the way toward becoming invisible and cynical. By rejecting parts of myself I damaged my spiritual and emotional health.

Self-awareness, integration of things we once disbelieved or disowned, leads to deeper awareness of God and life that fosters spiritual maturity, trust, and joy. We can't truly love others, or ourselves, if we don't know how to fully receive

and experience Divine Love. If we've experienced love as
pressure rather than communion it will be more difficult to
experience the deepest joy of unity or emotional intimacy
with God, with life, with ourselves, with others. Sometimes
this process happens quickly, as in "aha" moments of insight
or release; more often the peeling or discovery process is slow
and ongoing.

Fast-forward sixty years from the cat story. Mom is now
in her mid eighties, struggling with dementia, and aghast over
every one of her lost abilities, including writing and even
drawing a straight line. Amazingly, she can still verbally communicate. In an effort to give her a voice, and in my hopes
to catch some of her life stories before we lose them forever,
I assist her in journaling. With eleven children scattered all
over the world Mom wrote many letters, but she never kept a
personal diary or gave much significance to her own thoughts
and emotions. So when I get our journal out she becomes shy.

At first she tells only jokes or silly things for me to write
down. Humor is her way of dealing with discomfort and with
not being sure her memories are correct. Eventually, encouragement to tell the story as she can remember and the fa-
miliarity of this routine comfort her; she relaxes and begins
talking about her life. This morning as conversations often
go, one story leads to another, and because the past is easier
to remember than the present, Mom tells me a story I never
heard before.

She describes the humiliation of doing domestic chores
for other men while Dad was out of state, and how after a
short time of marriage, she had barely adjusted to being a
wife and mother and Dad's name came up for the draft. As
a conscientious objector, Dad chose to move to Marlboro,
New Jersey, and work in a state-run mental hospital rather
than serving in the military. Grieving the separation from Dad
and raising her first child alone, Mom says she had to find
work to support herself and son, Jimmy. She was small and
reserved and very young and inexperienced with life outside
her church and family world. Mom mentions how nervous

she was working for men who lost their wives and needed childcare or were unmarried and needed help with house and barn chores. The men were probably feeling awkward themselves; Mom shares how they barked out orders or mumbled directions. She stops, stares at the gold rocking chair across the room and I fear she's retreated into the maze that is her mind. One glance at her face shows she is not lost. I feel the depth of her remembering. Time must have moved agonizingly slow for her back then. When she continues the words come fast. Her hands flutter helplessly as she watches my furious scribbling. She talks about spilled milk pails, wails from her baby stuck in a playpen in a strange barn, burned meals from new stoves in unfamiliar kitchens, and her shame and exhaustion.

With her hands suddenly still, Mom tells me a woman's job became available in the same hospital where Dad worked. Overjoyed, she and Jimmy joined Dad. Mom's eyes shine remembering her anticipation. They could be together when off duty, but Jimmy would have to be in day care while they both worked. At the time it seemed so providential, so hopeful, and it seemed to be a real escape from her suffering. Mom falls silent again; I put down the pen and journal, tuck them out of sight, and take her hand.

The work in New Jersey is just misery in another form. She tells me how the male patients threatened her. Towering over her, and strong, they had few inhibitions and were often on drugs that made them belligerent before turning them passive. Mom, a tiny, submissive, Pennsylvania Dutch woman with no hospital training and certainly no street smarts, had to clean their rooms and strip their beds, both of which the men guarded fearlessly. They squirreled away food and forbidden items in corners and under mattresses.

If this wasn't difficult enough, every day Mom had to pass my toddler brother in the play yard as she went from one building to another. Traumatized by the separation, he always ran along the fence crying for her. She always scurried as fast as she could past him while keeping her head turned away. She couldn't look at my crying brother. I was horrified and fascinated by this story but instantly knew why Mom did this. She thought she was protecting my brother from further trauma. She thought not looking made the pain easier for him and thus easier for her to bear. Mom was not able to be present to such pain, hers or her children's, because she had no coping tools, except to "look away."

My heart breaks for her. I ache for her suffering, for my brother's suffering; I even ache for the ways I surely minimized my own children's growing-up traumas. I ache for myself too, remembering my cat story and the pain of Mom "turning away." I had thought she didn't care, which also meant God didn't care either. Instead, she had cared so deeply she feared being overwhelmed. Hearing her perspective shed new light on mine. Right then, my inner child experienced God as a deeply caring Mother.

I continued to sit, silently and tenderly stroking Mom's hand. With tears in our eyes, we smiled at each other. Mom's mind struggled with details in the telling of this story, but her soul spoke so eloquently. In listening deeply to her, without breaking the momentum by voicing any of my own commentary, we entered a deeper space, a sacred place of love, openness, and healing.

Though dementia brought so much frustration and sorrow to Mom and our family, I recognize the poignant blessing that came with it for me—the lowering of her guardedness, and thus, a window to her tender, beautiful soul. I value the times of deeper connection with her and Dad during those years, especially since it wasn't so available to me when I was growing up. Most of us intuitively know we are made for this kind of loving connection. Amid all the doing and earning, we long for emotional intimacy and connection because it sustains our souls. Most of us neither experience enough of this deeper sharing with others nor do we easily find places offering safety or guidance in how to be real with each other and tender with our stories.

Though I don't remember who said this statement—our stories are as sacred to God as God's stories are sacred to us—I do remember how it impacted me as a student in spiritual formation. It sounded scandalous and intriguing! Does God actually honor my story as much as I honored all the stories of God I heard since childhood? Do I believe in such a generous God, a God so loving that I, along with each person, am invited toward mutual sharing and sacred honoring of all our experiences? It is still intriguing for me to imagine how our churches, small groups, families, and work places would transform if we all believed that simple statement.

How can we treat our stories as sacred? How do we respect our journeys, our processes, our spiritual seeking and stumbling? Is it possible to be more open and free, less demanding or cynical? Yes, it is! We start by noticing all that is arising in us with compassion and without the normal judgmental, pressuring, labeling inner commentary. When we begin honoring our own emotional responses to life, letting them be there without repressing, judging, or fanning what arises, we honor our humanity. As we are able to be gentle with ourselves we are more likely to tell our stories to God. As we learn to fully allow God to love us, as we hold all our feelings and experiences in the presence of Love, we improve our ability to hold and honor the stories of others. This process heals us, peels us, releases our bonds and blinders, and helps us offer freedom to others.

Sharing all of life, both the honest struggle and the easy, leads us to communion and intimacy. Every human being suffers as well as rejoices; often, sharing the heavier things binds us more quickly than sharing only the good and positive in our lives. Emotional and spiritual intimacy calls us to keep our faith journeys honest and real. Many youth and young adults refuse to wear the good "church faces" so required of past generations. They know people who project constant happiness or strive for continuous tidiness in Christian living don't live in the real world and can't offer much hope to those whose lives are messy or whose hearts are broken.

There is freedom, healing, and genuine human connection when we can share our pain and stand in solidarity with each other without qualifying what is pain and what is suffering. Whenever we can listen and hold each other's stories without needing to add our own commentary on those stories, we honor the storyteller. Respecting each other's stories makes it safe for us to reveal our own, makes it safe to be real.

God hears and keeps our stories reverently because they matter. So often we are raised being told to be and think a certain way, and we do so to please authorities, which then becomes our response to God. We whitewash ourselves to look good in God's presence. This reminds me of a verse Mom tended to quote if she tired of us complaining: "whatever is true, whatever is noble, whatever is right, whatever is pure, whatever is lovely, whatever is admirable—if anything is excellent or praiseworthy—think about such things" (Philippians 4:8). She applied it to us as it was applied to her, probably, as a way of silencing childish dislikes. If the stage is already set for judging some thoughts and emotions as negative, the verse is more forceful than loving. I'm not a theologian, but I now understand this purity of thought is the fruit of continued spiritual practice. One has to understand the practice, the struggle, before it becomes possible to let go of dislikes and choose joy. So often we rush past the wrestling that needs our attention first.

I realized I couldn't ask my own children to let go of something I didn't allow them to own. So, when they were upset, I tried to honor their feelings by helping them put language around their experience. The whole process was inefficient and messy and usually happened when I was pressed for time! I got impatient as do all parents, but hopefully a blueprint toward emotional and spiritual health was drawn into the rough sketch of their lives.

In my childhood, music and song gave me some language for emotions and intimacy with God. I could sing about things I was not encouraged to verbally or affectionately express. Each generation builds on the experiences of the last one, and I applied my parents' ability for intimacy through music toward deeper expressions of my own experiences, whether singing or writing or communicating. I don't always exhibit emotional and spiritual health, but I want to keep growing in that direction as it will bring freedom, mellowness, and an undercurrent of joy that flows deeper than happiness. This joy, this centering in Love, this knowing that my story is held sacredly in the heart of God, keeps me moving from cynicism to joy.

CHAPTER 2

Rotten Grain and Filthy Lucre

WHEN TO HOLD, WHEN TO LET GO (SHARON)

When visiting our house, the grandchildren like to pile their favorite toys in heaps under the dining room table and sit amid their treasures. Our small grandson once put a huge pile of toys and books under the toddler table. He gathered until he was satisfied, and then became upset when there was no room for him to sit under the table with his stuff.

I have a small dachshund, Wren, with a similar problem. Wren hoards, snatches, and steals anything dropped or left unguarded. She carries toys and bones to her cuddle bed behind my chair. I no longer use our dog toy box; when the other dogs want a toy they go to Wren's den. I look there to find bottle caps, bag clips, and other things I've lost. Her pile of stuff gets so high she has to lie on top of everything or dig a hole for sleeping.

One night we forgot Wren was in her den chewing a bone. As we turned off lights for the night, Wren stumbled out with a large marrowbone stuck on her muzzle. In the dark, I rushed to help, grabbed the bone, and pulled, but it didn't budge. My efforts lifted Wren's front legs off the ground but the bone remained stuck. Baffled, I picked her up, switched on the light, and saw her tiny muzzle was not stuck in the hollow bone. She was gripping the bone in her teeth! We easily laugh at the antics of children and dogs, but they are humorous reminders of our own struggle to know when we have enough, when to hold on, and when to let go.

I know what it is to be in need, and I know what it is to have plenty. I have learned the secret of being content in any and every situation, whether well fed or hungry, whether living in plenty or in want. I can do all this through him who gives me strength.

—Philippians 4:12-13

JUST ENOUGH (DON)

I, as stated earlier, grew up in a family of eleven children. For most of my childhood, my father worked for a little more than the minimum hourly wage, and my mother, with all the children, had more than enough to do at home without entering the workforce to supply extra income. We had a small plot of land that provided vegetables and a cow to provide milk and other dairy products.

I always dreaded the beginning of school after Christmas vacation because of the question, "What did you get for Christmas?" The fact was we got mostly practical gifts like underwear or socks. I was embarrassed to tell my schoolmates about these gifts. There was just not enough money for superfluous items like toys and the other things my friends bragged about. One year, using personal money I had collected from a paper route, I bought myself an electric train set for Christmas so that I could brag about my "gift" to my friends.

In spite of an austere upbringing and my experience with Christmas, I seldom felt deprived or dissatisfied with my material possessions or unmet needs. We had all the essentials, and I didn't look to attain things beyond my own ability to acquire through my paper route, or the occasional dollar I was given for doing something extra for my parents.

When I think of my own experience with feelings of scarcity or abundance and compare them to my children's generation, there couldn't be a wider gap. Most of my children's peers were never satisfied with what they had. They were always looking for something else to acquire and it had to be the right brand. And no matter what was acquired, when the newest version came out, it was necessary to acquire it immediately, whether money from their allowance was enough or not. And most parents acquiesced to their children's demands.

Cravings and Hoarding
Although my financial situation has been better than that of my parents, my wife and I tried to raise our children with the same values that I had grown up with. We tried to have them compare themselves to those who had less rather than to those who had more. We volunteered in various ways, including a stint of service overseas. In many ways, we were more deliberate in teaching our children to be satisfied with what they had than my parents were. Their influence was out of necessity, while ours was out of choice.

So what made the difference? I think that more than anything else, it is the astute nature of modern advertising that creates needs where there aren't any to put us in a state of "perpetual dissatisfaction," as Mary Jo Leddy called it in her book *Radical Gratitude*.[1] She goes so far as to claim that our yearnings for the holy are supplanted by our thirst for things. "Through advertising, these spiritual desires are diverted and converted into cravings—for things, for a lifestyle rather than a life, for what is doomed to obsolescence rather than for what endures."[2]

I was probably less dissatisfied than my peers because our family did not have television during my childhood and teenage years. My desires were for simple things: a new bicycle which I was able to purchase with money from my paper route, a new transistor radio with which I could listen to my beloved baseball team and the top ten hit parade of songs, and a baseball glove. The only brand-name clothes we knew were Sears, Roebuck, and J. C. Penney. There was little need to buy music and replay it. There were few electronic devices to yearn for.

Not so today. We crave more and more things. Leddy writes: "Ours is a culture constituted through craving. It works as long as people want more, want to go shopping, want to think that freedom has to do with the range of choices available to the shopper. Without consumption there would be no production—and no profit."[3] In order to create the cravings in us, the advertising industry spends untold amounts of money and talent. The limitless choices, symbolized by the breakfast cereals I wrote about in the introduction, create in us cravings that we substitute for our real longing for God. Our god becomes our consuming.

Not Enough! Let Me Hoard!

Walter Brueggemann takes the idea even further in his book *Deep Memory Exuberant Hope*. He relates our craving to our belief in scarcity, again perpetuated by the advertising industry. "We never feel that we have enough; we have to have more and more, and this insatiable desire destroys us," he writes. "Whether we are liberal or conservative Christians, we must confess that the central problem of our lives is that we are torn apart by the conflict between our attraction to the good news of God's abundance and the power of our belief in scarcity."[4]

It is interesting that in spite of a conservative's common emphasis on morality and personal piety, the sin of overconsumption and dissatisfaction is seldom condemned. Likewise, the liberal's concern for social justice seldom extends to over-consumptive habits, many of which create much of the exploitation of other people's resources and hopes.

Brueggemann writes about God's provision of manna for the children of Israel in the desert: "Three things happened to this bread in Exodus 16. First, everybody had enough. But because Israel had learned to believe in scarcity in Egypt, the people started to hoard the bread. When they tried to bank it, invest it, it turned sour and rotted, because you cannot store up God's generosity."[5]

Saving for a rainy day is not all bad, even if that is what Bruggemann seems to suggest. It's the obsession with accumulation and the lack of trust in God that is bad. Are we more willing to believe in Pharaoh's hoarding and defense of that hoarding than in God's provision of enough manna for our needs? Hoarding and lack of trust leads to rotting and death.

David Fouche calls this culture of scarcity and hoarding "toxic." He uses the economic crisis of 2008 as evidence of this toxicity. "The recent Great Recession, which has so dramatically destabilized the world's economies, perfectly illustrates the fruits of toxic culture. The sheer greed that created the crisis is at the heart of this way of life."[6] The hoarding was not of grain that turned rotten, but of filthy lucre. Both Pharaoh and the bankers exhibit the acquisitive hoarding reality of Brueggemann's tale of death. As stated before, this toxicity is evidenced by our constant longing and dissatisfaction and perpetuated by the advertising industry and its skillful manipulation of us.

Unfortunately, this constant dissatisfaction and craving leads to more than acquiring material goods. According to Leddy, craving leads to "a general dissatisfaction with other people, with one's work, with the world, and with one's church or religious tradition."[7] This is a tale of death as well.

Be Grateful

Nearly every writer on spirituality agrees that the antidote to the craving and longings of the world of scarcity is gratitude. In this book we dedicate a whole chapter to gratitude, but an attitude of gratefulness cannot be emphasized enough in our acquisitive and hoarding culture. Opening our hearts for a new spirituality means turning a life of craving into a life of gratitude. Trying to fill our cravings with more things instead of God is idolatry and worshiping the god of mammon.

Mellowness of heart means turning Pharaoh's scarcity into God's abundance: choosing the tale of life over the tale of death. It also means turning the dissatisfaction and cravings of a toxic culture into gratitude. Doing these things has to be deliberate. Henri Nouwen writes: "Gratitude as a discipline involves a conscious choice."[8] We must choose to be grateful. And choosing to be grateful means not taking anything for granted. One of the greatest gifts we have is life itself.

Grateful for Life

Nowhere is this point made better than in Leddy's book *Radical Gratitude*. She writes about her own birth and how a nearly missed ferry could have meant that her father and mother wouldn't have met to conceive her. The miracle of this chance meeting fills her with gratitude. "Radical gratitude begins when we stop taking life for granted," she writes. "It arises in the astonishment at the miracle of creation and of our own creation."[9]

My own life is a miracle and a cause for gratitude. I nearly died three times in my childhood. When I was two years old I developed a very high fever with convulsions. According to the doctor, one more convulsion could have been fatal for me. When I was seven years old I slipped into a lake at a family reunion and nearly drowned. Only quick action by an older cousin who spotted a tuft of hair sticking out of the water saved me. Finally, at age eleven, my burst appendix caused an abscess to form in my abdomen and once again my frail body teetered between life and death. The fact that I am alive and quite well today fills me with a sense of gratitude.

It is unfortunate that there are so many more examples of resentfulness in our culture than gratitude. This resentfulness is more than likely the result of an unfulfilled sense of entitlement and the continual attempt to fill spiritual longings with amassing material goods. In order to combat this sense of entitlement and this resentfulness, we need to proclaim that enough is enough.

Enough Is Enough

When I was a new professor at a private school with a modest salary, a young man from my class approached me with an offer that he thought I couldn't refuse. He was an older student who was married and was trying to find ways to support his family and pay for his education. He decided to be a sales representative for one of the companies that uses a pyramid sales scheme. He began his pitch to me by saying that he knew that I wasn't making much money, and that I probably could use some extra income. He outlined how much people make through his company, and how much more I could make if I recruited people to work under me. My modest salary could be doubled, and he talked about all the nice things I could afford, including the trips back to Latin America where I had served as a missionary. The spiel was perfectly designed to lure those infected by our toxic culture of wanting more and not knowing when enough is enough.

Because of having lived in Latin America, and because of having experienced firsthand the oppression and poverty of many of my friends there, I had taken a vow of simplicity, however inconsistent. From somewhere deep within my soul I came up with this answer for my student. "I don't think I need more money," I said to him. "I am already a poor steward of the resources God has given me, and I don't want to be tempted by more." My student was left speechless. His script, prepared to tempt those infected by toxic culture, had no response for someone who didn't want more. It just wasn't normal.

I didn't know it at the time, but I was affirming God's abundance instead of Pharaoh's scarcity. I was declaring that enough is enough. At the end of the year, I received an anonymous note from a student. By the handwriting I knew whom it was from. "Keep doing what you do, professor Clymer," he wrote. "You are making a bigger impact on your students than you realize."

Blessed Are the Poor in Spirit

My journey with our toxic culture has been a tumultuous one. I was profoundly affected by the time I spent in Latin America, trying to sort through what was the authentic voice of God regarding values and what was from my culture. Through this struggle, I wrote a book on the Beatitudes, using stories of marginalized people as the examples Jesus spoke of in the Beatitudes. The first one on poverty, whether Luke's version of material poverty or the Matthew one on poverty of spirit, has always haunted me, especially in light of our materialistic culture. In writing about the poor man in my story for the beatitude I say, "The poor man realized his dependence on God and his neighbors, and lived in gratitude, knowing that he did not belong to himself." This surrender to God, to God's abundance and providence, is what helps to make us grateful, and helps us be cured of our cultural toxicity. "Self-surrender, ego surrender, and self-abandonment are not easy in any culture, and certainly more difficult in our individualistic one. Nevertheless, the more I can learn to abandon my own wants and needs and surrender to God, the more I will be able to become poor in spirit."[10]

An open heart recognizes God's abundance in the face of Pharaoh's scarcity. Such a heart surrenders to God's abundance and learns to be grateful for it. The heart learns to say that "enough is enough," and swims against the cultural current of acquisitiveness and hoarding. A spacious heart chooses the tale of life and gratitude rather than the tale of death—the tale of rotting grain and filthy lucre.

❧

EXPERIENCING GOD: LETTING GO OF INTERNALIZED FEARS OF SCARCITY (SHARON)

Some basic human needs are food, safety, and affection. I can easily imagine our hunter-gatherer ancestors crowding around empty fire pits when game was scarce and rains were not abundant. My belly rumbles with the children gathered there, seeing no spears full of roasting rabbit, only small bowls of meager seed and shriveled berries. Deep within our collective subconscious are memories of scarcity: famines, wars, droughts, pestilence, and the Great Depression. Given our history as humans, I understand our want of more. I have compassion on my own compulsions toward consumerism, buying, or storing up in fear of scarcity.

Unlike my brother, I grew up experiencing scarcity. Though we were well provided for, I came away from childhood with deeply etched experiences of not having enough and not being enough. I am the eighth child in our sibling lineup of eleven. Being younger and female, fewer resources were available to me. I remember my salivating anticipation as a plate of roast beef was passed around our large table. The platter started with Dad, was passed to his right for the older brothers to partake, then to the older sisters, until finally turning the corner to the left side of the table where the youngest ones sat. I waited patiently for my turn, knowing the working men were entitled to the biggest pieces. Meat was scarce in my experience.

When I wanted cereal with a banana, like advertised on TV, I was told bananas were only for men who packed their lunches to go to work. I was told the same if I asked for a snack of luncheon meat or sliced cheese. If I asked for a glass of orange juice, I discovered it too was only for those who ate a hearty breakfast before work. Now, I realize I was too compliant a child, as many of my other sisters didn't ask permission; they just got what they wanted and ate. Whether my view is the truth or what I alone experienced in our family, still, I can say I knew scarcity.

I experienced emotional scarcity as well. My family loved each other but didn't indulge in extravagant affection or emotional connection. We laughed and sang heartily, but we didn't share hugs, tears, fears, or compulsions. In my childish perception, stoicism and hierarchy ruled. Dad wielded the most power, then Mom, then older brothers, then sisters according to birth order. Of course circumstances sometimes switched this order. Parents and elders "got the floor" or were respected and expected to bring conversation or entertainment to our family unit. Older males especially, but also the more popular siblings, had the most status, voice, and food. As an introverted child in the midst of more extroverted, charismatic siblings, I grew up with internalized notions of scarcity and fear of not being enough. The world did not always feel safe for me.

As an adult raising a family and making a living from a small family farm, there were times of real scarcity, when crops failed, animals took ill, and weather was unmerciful. I have compassion for the internal struggle that happens when income is tight and it's hard to discern true need from want. Then and now, I find balance by looking around at the world to realize how blessed I am. Gratitude helps me move from that internalized scarcity mode to thankfulness and abundance.

Last summer, my friend joined me for dinner around our patio table. I found myself bemoaning our current struggle, and how difficult it was for my husband to find a complementary off-the-farm job that coordinated with his own farming schedule. I wished our farm contained more land so my husband could do the grain farming he loves instead of needing to track down some kind of job that is less fulfilling. When I paused, she looked at me with a strained expression.

"Look at this beautiful, old stone house of yours," she said longingly, eyes taking in the massive east side of our two-hundred-year-old stone house. "Wealth is relative, isn't it?" I fell silent, deeply challenged by her look, her gentle statement. I was speaking out of my old fears of scarcity. She extended grace listening to me, especially in light of her own bankruptcy declaration years ago. I followed her gaze to the sprawling hundred-year-old wisteria vine hugging the stone wall. Whenever someone expresses intrigue with our house, I feel renewed awe that we are the fourth Landis generation calling this place home and that my husband and his father were born here.

I can just as easily recite my frustrations with all this house lacks: electrical outlets, high enough ceilings for tall people, large rooms for big family gatherings, and closet space. The lack of closets alone feels tight and sparse to me.

Yet, sitting there looking up at my house through the yearning eyes of my friend, I connected deeply with all the "haves" of this place: history, stability, beauty, and character. Once an inn, this house sheltered weary travelers, and innkeepers hosted celebrations. Our divided upstairs used to be one whole room: a ballroom with a fireplace at each end and boot heel marks on the floor where men and ladies stood at the bar. Then there is the attic with odd nooks and crannies and the basement with a cool, dark arch cellar perfect for storing preserves and root vegetables.

I sometimes imagine the abundance of stories these old walls could spill. A sense of rootedness fills me, knowing generations of folks have shared love and belonging, work, laughter, prayers, sweat, and tears here. As a small link in this chain of ancestors, saints, rascals, historical figures, and present inhabitants, I feel incredibly grateful. With fertile land and our green thumbs, we will never starve. Two centuries of wind and storms have not destroyed this house yet, so safe shelter might be a given. I have enough to live well here. Besides, wherever I dwell, whatever my material status, I really want to believe in the overall abundance of God's created cosmos. I want my identity and security to rest in God.

My fear of scarcity suddenly became humorous. I laughed, startling us out of our pensiveness. We spent the evening talking about our needs, wants, fears, and blessings; our conversation, honesty, and laughter mellowed my heart.

Prayer, authenticity of others, and reflection on life circumstances help my subconscious fears arise to awareness. Then, with God's grace, I gain the freedom to embrace a spirit of abundance and gratitude.

Experiencing God: Connected to a God of Abundant Possibilities

"Mom, you need to *slam* the door!" Laughing, my daughter Stephanie helped me shut the heavy doors of our vacation home. This enchanted thatched-roof cottage with cheery red double doors rested atop a grassy hill among weathered boulders and sea pinks on the north coast of Ireland. My daughters ran ahead to take part in our early morning ritual of rushing outside to watch the sun rise. We could hardly settle to sleep each night, anticipating the light show as we stood at the edge of stony cliffs, amid wildflowers and sheep paths, buffeted by wind and sometimes rain, hearing waves crash against rocks below.

Each morning, I sprinted after the girls through both doors, slamming them behind me, only to hear loud banging as the Irish wind flung the doors back against their frames. The outer door had two halves and complicated latches. Much to the amusement of my daughters, one of them always had to help me wrestle the inner door closed and then properly shut both halves of the outer door.

The door closing became part of our daily routine, causing much laughter as we gathered to marvel at the beauty of each new day. After standing awed by the colors of Donegal at dawn, we'd go back inside and warm ourselves by the peat fire, enjoying tea and breakfast while studying tour books and planning our day. Then we'd pack our day bags and go outside for one more check of the weather. When heading out on such trips, Kim, keeper of keys, made sure she was last out of the cottage to close doors and lock up.

This particular morning, bags already piled on the table in front of us, we lingered over our cups of tea, watching wind and rain slam against the window. We waited for a lull in the weather, feeling sluggish. Kim suggested a short, fast run around the cottage to wake us up. Stephanie and I leaped up and raced to the doors, not bothering to grab coats or hats. Last again, I flew through the set of doors, determined to succeed in shutting the door behind me. Without breaking my pace, I held top and bottom door parts and slammed.

"I did it!" I bellowed jubilantly when both halves remained closed. The girls stopped, turned, cheered, and clapped in celebration. Suddenly, a sense of dread dropped like a rock in my gut. I yelled loudly above the roar of wind and waves. "Kim, do you have the house key?" Confused, Kim dropped her hands and searched her jeans pockets.

"No, it's in my coat pocket inside," she yelled back. "Why?" I watched her expression change as the same dread sank in her gut. I turned back to the door and yanked. It remained firmly closed. Kim pushed past me and gave the knob a hefty crank. Door and knob didn't respond. We laughed nervously.

"Good grief, Mom," Stephanie exclaimed. "First time you're successful in shutting the doors and you lock us out!" Our predicament became hilarious; we doubled over in laughter. Here we were, three mostly untraveled farm women traipsing around abroad. I guess beginner's luck was no longer our fourth companion. Kim felt optimistic; this couldn't be worse than learning to drive on the opposite side of the road. Talk of the car brought hope; we rushed to the car, simultaneously yanking on three different doors—all locked. We stood in a huddle, unconsciously pulling our sweaters tighter around us. Kim and Stephanie speculated about hidden keys and finding a way in.

"Okay, you two check windows and I'll look for hidden keys," I told the girls. We spread out, girls pushing and prodding each front window, while I lifted and looked under every mat, rock, and bush. It seemed we'd underestimated Irish determination in keeping out weather and intruders. Driving into Cruit Island, we had been thrilled to see no one around but us, a fact not in our favor now.

Alone at the back of the cottage, my spirits sagged. My mind picked at thoughts. *This is not going to end well.* Fear uncurled within me. *I'm not the carefree, spontaneous type. I'm scared for us. I like order and control, believe Murphy's Law, and think God is sometimes stingy.* Ah, there it was; another tendril of childish belief in a grudging deity that I had to find and discard. This situation asked me which belief I wanted to embrace, a God who "drops the other shoe" to test us, who usually withholds, or a God of love, limitless possibility, and abundance.

In the months before my trip, I'd practiced witnessing my dislikes without judgment, in an attempt to not over-identify with them. This witnessing gave me space to choose a response to the dislikes rather than simply reacting out of fear, anger, or entitlement. Doing this spiritual practice helped me be more present and less judgmental.

As soon as I noticed my disgruntled inner chatter, I eased into the thought-witnessing practice. My mind was racing. *This is entirely my fault! I've put my daughters in danger. I'm scared.* As I simply noticed and let the thoughts be, my soul quieted. My options for response were clear. I could receive the grace to trust the created world was as full of generosity and abundance as with difficulties and scarcity. I could open myself to possibilities or dwell on fear.

I chose grace and possibilities. Nothing changed, but I knew God's presence. I looked around and saw beauty in the craggy rock scapes, the wind and sky, wild flowers, shells, and snails that lined every footpath. I was glad my daughters were not angry with me and grateful for the sweaters we put on and the laughter we enjoyed. I thanked the clouds for easing their downpour into drizzle and thanked the sun for rising. *Oh my goodness; we're having an adventure in Ireland!* I didn't need to beg God for help or demand a miracle. It was enough to know that whatever happened, God was with us.

The girls and I regrouped; we accessed what we had, what we needed. We needed the cottage owner's contact information. We had hope, energy to walk for help, and the clothes on our backs. There was rugged terrain under our feet, and we were exposed to the raw weather that was Ireland in the spring. We scanned the landscape. Seeing the cottage-dotted hills around us, we went in separate directions to peer in windows and look for signs of inhabitation or entrance.

Stephanie shouted and we raced to her, thrilled at the sight of a car in front of one cottage. Suddenly shy about bothering the people inside, we hesitated. A gust of chilly wind gave us courage. A few knocks later, a sleepy man opened the door. He replied to our awkward introductions by shaking his head, looking at his female companion who told us they were German and her English was not good. Kim communicated with lots of hand gestures.

Despite language difficulties, they understood our need and produced their cottage rental agreement with directions to the owner's house. We thanked them profusely and headed for the door, preparing for the long, chilly walk ahead of us. The woman stopped us; the couple exchanged a torrent of German. She jangled their car keys. He looked uncertain, but soon shrugged on his winter coat and motioned us out the door. We piled into their small car. The windows promptly steamed up from all the adrenaline.

He was shy now, apologizing for his poor stick-shift driving skills. We smiled reassuringly, giddy with relief. After finding the owner's house and listening to her motherly concern, we had an extra key and piled back into the little rental car. On the ride back, I pondered kindness and generosity. Does believing in a generous God pave the way for generosity in me? Does a more generous spirit attract generosity from others? Does believing in a stingy God lean our energies toward being tightfisted and tight hearted?

Our German rescuer dropped us off at our cottage. We tested the key, opened our door, and waved exuberantly as he backed out our driveway. Drained, we fell into the benches around our table. Kim made tea and we quietly shared one more cup before heading out for the day. We were full of gratitude, knowing other ways this day could have unfolded.

My gratitude was not because I prayed and God delivered a happy ending. It was for the grace to want something deeper, for the willingness to risk becoming aware of my own weaknesses in order to stretch toward greater freedom and wholeness that celebrates God's abundance. Whether outcomes are happy or not, whether my needs are met or not, I'm slowly beginning to know that softening toward trust, and experiencing God with me, is enough.

CHAPTER 3

In the Present Moment

HEIGHTENED AWARENESS DURING CHEMO (SHARON)

I was officially bald, except for the prick of stubble Stephanie's clippers left on my head. My daughter was cheerful when clipping, while my husband, Jay, documented the process. I hadn't minded losing my hair, but at the first look of digital photos, I almost cried. Something about the poignancy of their tender, loving faces and their cheerfulness despite the seriousness of my illness, made the tears well up. I laughed though, at my square jaw and seeing more wrinkles than I thought I possessed. Seeing my new image took some adjusting.

I really liked the crew cut I had at first. Then my head began getting sore, waking me up at night, itchy and stinging. My hair was coming out with every shampoo and touch of a comb. It seemed logical to get rid of the hair and soak my head in anti-itch shampoo. I saved the teeny clumps. They all fit in a very small plastic container. What a sad, pathetic little pile of hair, as if Stephanie had clipped a mouse!

My friend Judy took me to try on wigs at the American Cancer Society center. I was allowed to pick three free items, but still dreaded the morning since I tend to get flustered with too many options. The women at the center were so cheerful and positive, it wasn't as overwhelming as I expected. I had fun! Judy and I laughed hysterically at my face under a punk rocker wig: black hair with spikes of blonde and red. After many tries and much laughter, I chose one brown-haired wig and two hats. I still want to go to a wig shop and find a wig that is more my natural hair color: a mixture of silver, brown, and blonde. It should be easy if I show the wig shop stylist my mouse-sized container of multicolored hair bits!

ह❧

Be ever hearing, but never understanding; be ever see-
ing, but never perceiving. Make the heart of this people
calloused; make their ears dull and close their eyes.
Otherwise they might see with their eyes, hear with their
ears, understand with their hearts, and turn and be healed.
—Isaiah 6:9b-10

Therefore do not worry about tomorrow,
for tomorrow will worry about itself. Each day
has enough trouble of its own. —Matthew 6:34

CROSS-CULTURAL EXPERIENCES HEIGHTEN AWARENESS (DON)

There were twenty-one of us—nineteen students and two leaders—sitting around a circle discussing a passage from Henri Nouwen's book *Gracias*. We were in the last two weeks of a semester-long sojourn through Guatemala and Mexico as part of a cross-cultural requirement for the university where I work. "The children always challenge me to live in the present," wrote Nouwen. "They want me to be with them here and now, and they find it hard to understand that I might have other things to do or think about."[1]

We had just come through an excruciatingly challenging but rewarding visit to Mexico City, and along with being tired, many of us were focused on our return home and meeting with significant others, family, and friends. It was particularly difficult to be focused on the present. Hence, Nouwen's words struck a chord. He continued, "I marvel at [the children's] ability to be fully present to me. Their uninhibited expression of affection and willingness to receive it pull me directly into the moment and invite me to celebrate life where it is found."[2] Children have a way of being continually surprised by what is happening now, in the present moment.

I asked my students to list what things they could do to remain present, to "celebrate life where it is found," to be surprised like children. Their list included three things: spending time in silence, making lists of interesting things they wanted to do each particular day, and staying focused on the relationships they developed with their host families, teachers, and fellow group members. As leaders, my wife, Esther, and I were impressed with their insightful list. The students provided us with an excellent beginning to learn how to function in order to balance our spirituality with a mellow heart.

Too Much Focus on the Past or the Future

According to Eckhart Tolle in his book *The Power of Now*, most of humankind's problems stem from the fact that our minds are in a constant state of worrying about either the past or the future with little consideration for the present moment.[3] He encourages his readers to live in the "now." By living in the past or the future we so often miss the miraculous happening right before our eyes. When we are unconscious, unaware, or not present, wonderful God-moments pass us by like shadows in the night. We can become childlike and open for surprises or miracles as we face each moment of the day. The present is where the temporal meets the eternal; we find

God in the present. This makes the present holy. This is why it is important to be present to the now, to the holy, to God.

The cross-cultural semester that I referred to provided examples of two extreme ends of the spectrum on presence and living in the now. The beginning of the story represents an extreme focus on the future—the desire to return home to the familiar. This thinking about the future makes one think about the past as well—how things were before the trip, both in terms of levels of comfort and relationships. These thoughts are normal but can become unhealthy when your whole thought life obsesses on the future and home.

One student was so focused on her home that her host mom in Mexico became quite concerned. She would not eat anything that was prepared for her, refused to speak Spanish—even if her ability in Spanish at the time was much above average—and was non-responsive to the extreme, walking about with the longest imaginable look on her face. At her wit's end, her host mom came to the administrator of the program to ask what she could do to make this student more responsive. The focus on going home and the resultant preoccupation with the past (probably over-romanticizing it) had completely overtaken our student's ability to function normally in her "present" situation. This extreme came near the end of our study-abroad experience.

In contrast, at the beginning of a cross-cultural experience students often exhibit a healthy example of presence and living in the now. I call this phenomenon "heightened awareness." A student who has never traveled outside her own country, or is experiencing a new country for the first time, has her senses completely attuned to the newness she is encountering: the new smells, the new sights, the new sounds all surround her with stimuli that keep her present to the moment—living in the now. There is little thought about the future or the past since the current moment is so profoundly engaging. There are few times in one's life where this "heightened awareness" is more acute than in circumstances such as entering a new culture, country, or experience. There are few times when one is so focused on the present.

Unfortunately, this heightened awareness is difficult to sustain after one has adapted to the new setting and things become more routine. The amount of focus on the present varies from person to person as the time abroad progresses.

One student was constantly concerned that he would miss out on an opportunity to make the most of his time in the country. He wanted every moment to be filled with new learning. We were at the end of our time in a particular area, and we were leaving by bus for our next learning center. Everyone had arrived early and we were all aboard the bus and ready to go some twenty minutes before the schedule said we were to leave. Our eager learner approached us and asked: "Are we leaving when the schedule says we are leaving, or are we leaving now? Do I still have 20 minutes?" he asked.

I thought he wanted to go to the bathroom, or to say goodbye to someone in the institute where we had been studying. Instead he replied to my inquiry, "There is one museum that I didn't have time to visit while we were here, and I wanted to see if I still had time to take it in." The rest of the students and the leaders were focused on the future—getting to the next place and the opportunities that awaited us there. He was still focused on the present time and place and wanted to get the most out of that moment. Few people have such a focus on the present, even at the beginning of a cross-cultural experience. Nevertheless, this is a wonderful example of how to live in the present.

Experiencing Loss Heightens Awareness

"Heightened awareness" also happens to most people when they experience a significant loss. When one loses a loved one through death, time stands still. One becomes totally focused on the present moment.

Nearly every writer on spirituality recognizes the potential for growth through loss. Nancy Copeland-Payton, in her article on loss, states, "healthy growth walks hand in hand with sometimes painful loss, for to let go of what was formerly life-giving cuts deep."[4] The deeper the cut, potentially, the higher the awareness and the growth one can experience.

The days leading up to my father's death and then planning his memorial service and burial were intense and painful times. Yet it seemed like my senses were amplified and I was aware of God's presence far more acutely than I had ever experienced it before. At the time I wrote, "Death, however final and sad it feels, brings love of family to the fore. It also shows how much we need the larger community of friends and the church. I love life more today than I did last week. And I love my family and my friends who have surrounded me with their care more than I did last week. And when that community stretches to many places in the world, it is even more special."

How could I say that I love life more than before when I had just experienced the death of my father? My heightened awareness helped me to find the miraculous in the moment. It helped me see the holy. It brought the eternal and the temporal together in the present.

It shouldn't take painful loss or a spectacular cross-cultural experience to learn to live in the now. One can develop blessed awareness through spiritual practices and also through awareness of the present—the portal to the miraculous and the holy.

No Worries about Tomorrow

Jesus said in Matthew 6:34, "Therefore do not worry about tomorrow, for tomorrow will worry about itself. Each day has enough trouble of its own." A spacious heart is not worrying about either tomorrow or yesterday. It is living in the moment, in the present, discovering that God is present in the now. This idea is repeated in both the Hebrew and Christian Scriptures. Earlier in the same chapter, Matthew gives a longer version of how to focus on the present rather than the future:

Therefore I tell you, do not be anxious about your life, what you will eat or what you will drink, nor about your body, what you will put on. Is not life more than food, and the body more than clothing? Look at the birds of the air: they neither sow nor reap nor gather into barns, and yet your heavenly Father feeds them. Are you not of more value than they? (Matthew 6:25-27)

Anxiety about tomorrow relates very closely to the abundance and scarcity discussed in chapter 2. When we center our thoughts on tomorrow we become concerned about not having enough, about being prepared for all the potential calamities that could befall us. Again, as with abundance and scarcity, the advertising industry knows how to exploit our fears and tries to assuage the anxiety with a myriad of products, most of which we don't need.

Jesus assures us that we are worth more than the birds and that God takes care of them. He also nudges us to live in the present by saying, "And which of you by being anxious can add a single hour to his span of life?" (Luke 12:25). There is abundant evidence that being anxious about tomorrow and the resultant stress actually subtracts hours from one's span of life. Anxiety is the opposite of mellowness. Corrie ten Boom wrote, "Worry does not empty tomorrow of its sorrow. It empties today of its strength."[5]

Focus on the Present

So how do we stay focused on the present? How do we develop "ears to hear and eyes to see" what God is doing presently with us in order to be mellow of heart? I go back to the list my students came up with on how to be present in their last weeks of the study-abroad program as a beginning point for our discussion:

1. Spend time in silence.
2. Make a list of interesting things they wanted to do that particular day.

3. Stay focused on the relationships they had with their host families, teachers, and fellow group members.

Silence

To spend time in silence is perhaps the most needed spiritual discipline of our time. It will be repeated throughout this book. It is also one of the most practiced disciplines among those who are serious about their spirituality.

I was first introduced to the idea of silence as a way to get in touch with my soul through the writings of the great Swiss psychiatrist Carl G. Jung. In his collected works, he tells the story of a stressed-out pastor who came to him for counseling. Jung's prescription for him was to spend eight hours a day doing his regular work routine, eight hours a day for sleep, and spend the final eight hours in silence. After several failed attempts to remain silent for so long, the pastor in desperation exclaimed to Jung that he would go crazy being alone with himself for so long. Jung didn't hesitate long in responding to the frazzled pastor that now he would understand how other people felt about being with him.[6]

Perhaps few of us could regularly endure eight consecutive hours in silence, but the lesson here is that if we do not get to know our own soul, we run the risk of projecting our worst selves onto others. Silence helps us to be aware of that inner and outer presence. It brings us back from our ego-dominated thinking about the future and the past and makes us present to the moment, helping to find the miraculous mellowness and openness of heart.

Ordinary Is Extraordinary

The second item on our students' list for staying present was to "make a list of interesting things they wanted to do that particular day." This was not a glorified to-do list. It contained something new and exciting to do in order to keep them present and focused on the moment. For our purposes, on the other hand, we need to look beyond solely the "interesting things." The person who is truly in the now, truly attentive to God's presence, can find God in the uninteresting and the mundane as well as the exciting things. So we are not to make a list of what we plan to see or do during the upcoming day, but rather to compose our list as we go along. "I saw God in the full moon hanging over the horizon on my walk this morning; I saw God in my breathing in rhythm with the pace of my feet; I saw God in the sidelong glance my wife gave me in the kitchen; I saw God in the Facebook message I received from a former student; I saw God in the smile of a child . . . " and an infinite number of similar mundane daily happenings. This is developing heightened awareness. This is developing "ears that hear and eyes that see." Then at the end of the day, we can go back over our day, reviewing the list in our "consciousness examen" (see glossary), and in gratitude give God thanks for these new areas of awareness.

Focus on Relationships

Finally on the student list is "stay focused on relationships." There is nothing so disconcerting than to be involved in a conversation with another person when they are not present. While you are telling your friend something which you deem to be very important, their eyes keep darting from place to place, and before you finish they break in with a response. We often plan our response instead of listening to what someone says.

Unlike the situation described above, when students are learning a new language on a cross-cultural experience, they are very present with the person with whom they are speaking. In order to understand, they listen very carefully to each word, not skipping ahead in their thinking, guessing what might be said. This concentration is very tiring, but it is also rewarding when one begins to get "inside the thoughts" of the other person, and hence gets a glimpse not only into the personality of the other person, but also into their culture. Once again, the intensity of a cross-cultural experience gives us the best example of being present, in this case in relationship with other people. If we could exert such concentration in all our relationships, we would indeed be present to them.

After these intense experiences with being fully present on their cross-cultural program, my students longed for deeper connections with their family and friends upon returning home. Many vowed to have one face-to-face conversation with a friend for every text message sent. Another added, "I want to be more grateful each day and be much more present with my family and friends."

ॐ

.... EXPERIENCING GOD: STARTING AT THE BOTTOM (SHARON)

When you cannot enjoy the lilies of the field or the
sparrows in the sky, don't waste time thinking you
can enjoy God. Start at the bottom; try to love a rock.

—RICHARD ROHR[7]

This quote amused me during a time when I really needed gentle, transforming humor, when I struggled to accept the "rocks" in my life: difficult people, circumstances, and schedules. My flower gardens did not even console me, as they too were full of glaring white rocks that wind and rain had surfaced. The rocks came from a load of stone-contaminated mulch we bought and spread on our gardens last season. As an avid rock admirer and collector, I felt completely out of sorts with my dislike of these rocks, even irritated at my irritation! Thus the catchy phrase found a home in my soul, tickling my mind and heart in a playful way, a welcome contrast to the other way—my mind's compulsive insistence to be more spiritual, to skip ahead to joy and peace, rather than first honoring and being completely present to the rocks, both literal and figurative.

Richard Rohr goes on to say,

we try to be spiritual before we have learned to be human. Maybe this is why Jesus came to model humanity for us—much more than divinity. Once we get the human part down, 'stop slamming doors' and start loving rocks, God will most assuredly take it all from there. Get the ordinary human thing down, and you will have all the spirituality that you can handle.[8]

Deepening my spirituality, including any successful mellowing of the heart, will be ongoing. Spiritual growth and faith development is like a spiral; often I find myself circling around a familiar issue going deeper each time around as self-deception becomes more subtle and gaining insight requires greater presence and compassion.

It comforts me knowing everyone struggles with rocks in their lives: inner turmoil and anxieties, or illness, loss, accidents, or financial stresses. No one is always laid back. Even spiritual giants have times of starting slowly at the bottom—perhaps loving rocks—when loving lilies, people, and God take too much energy. Despite frequent failure, I desire deep authenticity, where my interior impulses and thoughts match my exterior words and actions. Assimilating this will take an imperfect lifetime.

Oddly, I'm both an idealist and a realist. These aren't my only opposing energies; I'm also a people-pleasing, solitude-loving hermit. I enjoy silent alone time, yet I frequently crave companionship. Despite loving quiet, I'm easily bored and need deep or stimulating conversation or to experience new places and fun activities with friends or family. I'm a messy perfectionist. Silence and solitude show me the truth of myself and I'm moved with compassion for others who love me, and for my own humanity.

My speaking and writing will always contain both idealistic and visionary propensities as well as the more realistic tendency to simply stop trying so hard to be positive when life is challenging. I remember telling a pastor about my difficulties working with a particular person. In the telling, I struggled between wanting to speak frankly and wanting to remain positive. The pastor suggested I was being descriptive about the person and the situation, not negative or judgmental. It was a relief to speak candidly. When my infant grandson needed skull surgery, our family deeply appreciated others who heard our laments and fears without pressuring us to be positive or trust too quickly that everything would be fine. I want to be grateful in the midst of difficulties, yes, but not in place of clearly seeing and honoring what is difficult. The heart is more spacious when one is willing to stand in the trenches and mourn with those who mourn, not trying to convince the mourners to ignore the negative by shaming them into speaking only of the positive. In some mysterious way, the trenches belong too.

I don't have to like the trenches—the conflicts, losses, upheavals, medical emergencies—in order to be open hearted. There are times when I'm completely joyful and content even during unpleasant realities. Other times melancholy takes over. Mature spirituality is not one state over the other. It's not repressing strong emotions or tumultuous thoughts in hope of always peacefully enjoying lilies and sparrows, rocks, and God.

Spiritual maturity is being aware of and present to strong emotions and thoughts, and also being aware of God's goodness and beauty and resting in the midst of life's unrestful moments. Deeper spiritual awareness is holding paradoxes and opposites together, not judging one better or worse, not demanding, pushing, or forcing anything or anyone to change, but just being aware and alert, and discerning what is and what is not my own personal invitation toward action.

One of the worst injustices we do to people who are ill, grieving, or suffering is to want them to be strong and upbeat, especially spiritually, and be joyful right away. We fear our own bottoming out, should we ever suffer, so we almost demand others not show their depths of sorrow and loss or speak of times God feels distant. We glorify victory over endurance and being real. Spiritual maturity is emitting both strength and vulnerability.

My father exemplified this vulnerable strength while undergoing chemotherapy for chronic leukemia. Never one to complain or share much of his interior life, he still found ways to show us how he was experiencing life. He often spoke with much courage, welcoming chemotherapy and expressing his willingness to heal, while tears gathered in his eyes. His tears were neither weakness, nor his spoken courage a lie, but they were proof of his ability to be strong and vulnerable at the same time.

As a young father Dad could be angry and impatient, but I'll remember him most by his transformation as he aged. One experience remains etched forever in my mind. One day I found him lying flat on his back on the floor of his apartment. I had brought him a meal and pushed open his door when he didn't respond to my knock. He had fallen hours ago, his cell phone in his pocket but unreachable due to his position. He lay there weakened and in pain yet showing incredible grace. He was calm and present, thankful I had promised him dinner, and he did not utter a single word of self-condemnation for falling, regret I hadn't come sooner, or anger that no one heard him calling for help.

My greatest invitation toward heightened awareness, staying present, grateful, playful, and openhearted was during and after my bout with cancer in 2009. Many spiritual practices, like centering prayer and meditation learned at Kairos: School of Spiritual Formation before my diagnosis, were faith anchors for me during recovery.

When I was first learning about centering prayer, meditation was the hardest practice. It seemed so utterly pointless, so countercultural, unproductive, and foolish, but now I can truthfully say, there is nothing better for me than meditation and contemplative prayer. Both have long stopped being a discipline. Such times of quietly opening myself to life draws me, pulls me toward greater love and joy. I don't have to form words, or produce, or perform. All I have to do is quiet my mind, sit in stillness, and open myself to love, to God, to Christ, and to the Intelligent Creator of the cosmos.

While receiving chemo I listened to guided imagery CDs and drifted in and out of sleep and centering prayer. It was lovely feeling so calm, centered, and surrounded by love and healing. I felt all the energy, thoughts, and prayers coming my way. Spiritual teachers told me that students need to learn such disciplines when there are no demands or big stresses, and then when life brings struggle and difficulty, one can lean on already established practices. Of course I didn't quite believe them, especially when struggling to sit still, ignore my racing thoughts, itches, and tingles, or my arms or legs that were falling asleep. After five minutes I'd give up. Gradually, though, I experienced the truth of their teaching and centering prayer became a deep sigh of relief. I couldn't have faced the challenge of cancer with as much humor and grace without those life-balancing practices and disciplines. I could trust more than doubt—believe all could be well in my soul, even if not in my body or in the world.

My spiritual practice of staying present, openhearted, and centered in Divine Love, also helped me deal with suffering. Soon after the start of chemo, my tongue, throat, and hair cells began dying along with the cancer cells. Some good things had to be sacrificed along with the bad things. This reminds me, oddly, of love. When one chooses to live open and unguarded, surrendered to love, a few walls of defense need to come down: like seeing beyond physical beauty, seeing the spirit glowing rather than the face. I never thought myself beautiful, but I did define myself as "not bad looking." Each round of chemo brought lip blisters and angry zits, as if hair loss wasn't enough. Looking good is sometimes sacrificed in cancer healing. Strangely, I often felt beautiful during treatment; God's grace carried me even through glances in the mirror.

Love demands I love myself as much as others. I must love myself in the process of healing, where I am right now, not love myself when I've become what I want to be, or when I'm healed or worthy enough. God loves me right now, where I am in life's process. I am asked to do the same, for myself, for others. The time for love is right now, no matter what struggle or glory is happening within or around me.

A month before my diagnosis, my spiritual director quoted something that hit a deep chord. I remember smiling deeply, just receiving the quote into my soul. I can't remember who said this or if this is the exact quote: "It is a truly gracious person who wants what they get in life, rather than insisting on getting what they want." I'm still astounded that I was unaware that tumors were growing in my body then. The longing and desire to be so accepting of life was growing in me along with cancer. Is this how love expands my heart? Was this God preparing me for what was coming?

I don't believe the quote means passively living with an abuser, or putting up with what needs to be changed. I believe it means embracing "what is," that which can't be changed no matter if one stomps feet, yells, fights, denies, or runs. I've discovered God doesn't mind stomping or yelling. I've yelled at God plenty of times and thrown fistfuls of old eggs into our farm manure pit during periods of releasing anger. I imagined God clapping and egging me on. God is big enough to embrace my real feelings. Over the years, I've learned God loves when I'm real, when I own my emotions, face them, and deal with them in nonviolent ways. God becomes real to me in equal measure to how real I am with God.

No one welcomes cancer. Yet the spiritual path brings paradox; along with bad often comes good. Another quote from teachers at Kairos that I love is this: "To live is to grow. To grow is to change. To change is to suffer." Suffering is bearable when one can open to the gifts hidden within. The first gift I received during recovery was sudden clarity about my body, my life, and my desires. It's amazing how easily I've been able to separate what matters from what doesn't matter, and how I've learned to trust and let go of control.

Another gift was letting go of fear. I've carried within me a lifelong dream of writing for the public, but fear kept my writing hidden. Since cancer and chemo, death doesn't seem as far removed, and suddenly I am no longer bound by fear. My writing flows as before, but now I share instead of keeping it to myself. I share whether or not anyone approves. And I'm amazed when people do.

Others sustain me with their wonderful writings: "I stand before what is with an open heart and dwell in possibilities," says Macrina Wiederkehr.[9] My dictionary says equanimity means calmness or composure, and Jean Halifax's definition of equanimity is "the stability of mind that allows us to be present with an open heart no matter how wonderful or difficult conditions are."[10] Another memorable quote from Macrina Wiederkehr is "God, help me believe the truth about myself, no matter how beautiful it is."[11]

A year after my lymphoma diagnosis and four months of immuno-chemotherapy, when I was well into recovery and celebrating wonderful healing milestones, I still experienced bouts of melancholy. One lovely autumn day, needing some consolation, I took a walk, and then sat on my favorite bench on a hill overlooking a creek. The trees around me were ablaze in red, orange, and gold. The sun felt so good after days of rain. I felt blue, yet alive and alert. My mind skipped around from thought to thought, then relaxed deeply into spacious appreciation of earth's sights, sounds, and smells. Moments later, as thoughts returned, I felt momentarily confused—was this spring or autumn? I saw signs of spring: a swollen creek, curving like a ribbon over deep moss and cress, water spilling over banks as if fed by spring rains, green grass carpeting the ground before and around me. I looked up, reassured by golds and reds. Yes, it was autumn. Fields of yellow ripened corn were bordered by emerald strips of vigorously growing alfalfa. Rows of brilliant red burning bushes arose from lush lawns.

Like two eyes that see double when relaxed and single when focusing together, my exterior senses relaxed enough to sharpen my interior, deeper awareness. The melancholy blurred with joy until my thoughts and feelings became one with the pulse of life, the green earth, brilliant red leaves, golden corn, and flowing waters. I savored this simple, spacious moment, while holding it all lightly.

Such savoring helped me look for joy even while dreading my chemo medi-port removal procedure or other difficult life situations, sad endings, or unpleasant emotions. I joyfully anticipate a grandchild's smile, happy beginnings, and the bite of a crisp apple. These simple ups and downs symbolize the ebb and flow of change.

Then and now, life has seasons to be noticed and enjoyed, and holding everything lightly helps ease the transitions. It's a comfort knowing I'm not defined by my thoughts or emotions, by what happens in my life. My true self is deeper, wider, more connected to something bigger than myself. In joy or in disappointment, I can focus on my own state, or I can open to the pulse of humanity, of earth, sea, and sky, and the Spirit, too. One focus without the other tends to keep clinging or wishing for some other emotion, situation, state, or season.

I remember lying awake with my chest numbed, on the surgeon's table for the feared port removal, wishing to be asleep. How I prayed to see a bigger picture than my dread! My daughter-in-law, Elizabeth, told me to visualize the port covered in slippery butter so it would pop right out. I did, but unfortunately the port stuck and hurt coming out. Yet I found joy in the loving support of family and the hilarious look on the usually stoic surgeon's face when he thought I might faint mid-procedure—joy to breathe and move through, and hold it all lightly.

CHAPTER 4

Lessons from the Weeds
and the Flowers

BIRDS, BERRIES, AND INSTANT GRATIFICATION (SHARON)

Avery, my three-year-old granddaughter, followed me to the raspberry patch carrying her own small bucket. As we walked past the potted blueberries on our patio she asked me why they were covered in brides. Laughing, I explained that tulle is a fabric used to make fancy dresses like brides wear, but it's also useful for draping over berry bushes to keep birds from eating the berries. Birds love blueberries, and I don't like when birds eat all the berries before I get to taste them. She didn't say anything, just looked back over her shoulder at the shrouded blueberry bushes as we walked hand in hand to the garden.

I showed her how to carefully pluck the black, juicy raspberries from the tangle of thorny branches and we popped the first few in our mouths. We grinned with stained teeth. Under my supervision she continued picking and carefully placing each fat berry in her pail. When I was satisfied she was doing fine, I began picking myself. We worked in silence, enjoying the hot sun and sweet smells of summer. I glanced at Avery, hoping her bucket wasn't too full and the berries weren't squished, but I was surprised to see an empty pail. The happy child, with her mouth full and purple juice dripping off her chin, quickly explained: "Don't be sad, Nana. I'm just a tiny little birdie eating berries!" I laughed, delighted with her childish logic, and received her exuberance as gratitude.

໕

Enter his gates with thanksgiving and his courts with praise; give thanks to him and praise his name.
—Psalm 100:4

One of them, when he realized that he was healed, turned around and came back, shouting his gratitude, glorifying God. He kneeled at Jesus' feet, so grateful. He couldn't thank him enough—and he was a Samaritan.
—Luke 17:14b-16 (*The Message*)

.... GRATITUDE (DON)

The classic biblical story about gratitude is the story of the ten lepers who received healing and salvation from Jesus, recorded in Luke 17. Only one of the ten returned to thank Jesus for giving him back his life—an outsider at that. All ten were considered unclean because of their leprosy—outsiders. But the grateful man was a double outsider. Not only was he unclean, but also, as a Samaritan he was considered an enemy of the Jews.

What motivated the one to return? What kept the other nine from returning? Perhaps they had a sense of entitlement and took their healing for granted. Perhaps they were too distracted with their newfound health to remember who cured them. Perhaps they expected instant healing and gratification since they believed that Jesus was the Messiah. Perhaps one in ten is the normal average of grateful people that we can expect in any time and place. Whatever the reasons, the natural attitude flowing from the gratitude of the one leper was praise. A mellow heart ensues from such gratitude and praise.

Too Many Choices

Choices, choices, choices. I wanted to upgrade my cell phone. I didn't use it much but was intrigued by the possibilities of a smartphone. I also wanted to be free of the major phone companies and their two-year contracts. I had used a family plan with one of the major companies for many years, and every time I examined my bill closely (I mean reading the really fine print), I would discover that I was paying for much more than I was using, even on the minimum plan. After using a pay-as-you-go plan for my cell phone while abroad, I decided that was the way to go.

During the past number of years I had carried around an iPod touch, which acted exactly like an iPhone without the phone part. I had accumulated a number of applications for it that I really liked, so I wanted to buy an iPhone. So I tried to find a pay-as-you-go company that offered an iPhone. No such luck. I searched for plans and the accompanying phones and I could not believe the number of companies out there. It became obvious that the iPhone was only available through a large company with a minimum of a two-year contract, both of which I wanted to avoid. The iPhone was also by far the most expensive. So I needed to choose. *Do I find a phone with minimal capabilities and keep using my iPod touch? If I go with a smartphone, which one should I choose?* There were literally hundreds of possibilities for phones and plans.

So I spent hours online trying to decide which phone and company offered me the best value for the money. The more I tried to decide which was my best option, the more irritated I became. I simply had too much information and too many choices.

This simple illustration highlights the irritation of having too many choices for one little product. Yet practically everything we experience has choice involved—cars to drive, colleges to attend and majors to study, churches to join, or computers to use—the lists are endless. Unless we consume compulsively, each one of these choices requires a certain amount of deliberation, which raises the expectations and demands on our decision. Because our expectations are so high, we are invariably disappointed in our final decision and wish that we had checked out one more consumer report.

Having Choices Does Not Spell Happiness

We tend to think that having lots of choices improves our quality of life. Our whole socioeconomic system in the United States is based on that idea. If this were true, the United States would be the freest and happiest country in the world. Barry Schwartz's book *The Paradox of Choice* shows the fallacy of this cultural myth: "though modern [U.S.] Americans have more choice than any group of people ever has before . . . we don't seem to be benefiting from it psychologically."[1] In fact, instead of well-being and happiness, too many choices seem to cause resentfulness.

I have often taught my students that people living in the developing world suffer from too few choices, while people in the industrialized nations like the United States suffer from too many choices. Why is this so? According to Schwartz, when "opportunities [become] so numerous . . . we feel overwhelmed. Instead of feeling in control, we feel unable to cope."[2] One of the predominate cultural traits of U.S. Americans is the need to be in control. Losing control depresses us. When we finally make a decision, we second-guess our choice. "You're hit with a double whammy—regret about what you didn't choose, and disappointment with what you did."[3] If for some reason we are happy with our choice, that delight doesn't last very long because of a psychological phenomenon called *adaptation*. "Simply put, we get used to things, and then we start to take them for granted."[4] When we take things for granted, we raise our expectations even more, and when those expectations aren't met, we become resentful.

Taking things for granted must be the plague of any person of faith trying to live in the United States or any other industrialized country. According to Mary Jo Leddy in her book *Radical Gratitude*, "The longer we live ungratefully, the more we strengthen the claims of a culture that takes everything and everyone for granted."[5] How do we combat this attitude? The first lesson that I hope for students to learn who go on the semester-abroad programs I have led is not to take their privileges and comfortable lifestyles for granted. When they experience poverty and oppression in the countries we visit, they immediately express a desire to be more grateful and not to take things for granted.

When we (myself included) return home, however, it is much more difficult to maintain this attitude because of the phenomenon of adaptation that Schwartz wrote about. What was a positive feeling of accomplishment on our consumptive choice (my new cell phone), or a commitment to a different lifestyle (returning from an intense cross-cultural experience), turns sour. Satisfaction becomes dissatisfaction, frustration, or even anger because of adaptation. The irony of having too many choices, instead of making us happy, grateful, and more fulfilled, is that it makes us resentful.

I Want It Now

Nothing exemplifies our culture's need for instant gratification better than the use of credit cards. With a credit card, nearly anyone, including college students and the homeless, can purchase almost anything that suits their fancy whenever they want to. Until the credit card age, the person who amassed debt was considered an anathema to society, and having to declare bankruptcy was the gravest of sins. This has totally changed. There is little stigma attached to personal debt, and many people rack up debts with no intention of paying them off. The real problem is that people want to fulfill their current "need" immediately. Seldom do they examine the spiritual cost of their continual compulsive spending.

Instant gratification is a plague that is killing the spirituality of our culture. College students seem to be the most vulnerable to the wooing of credit card companies and the least remorseful about not paying accumulating debt. According to the website Credit.com, "The average number of [credit] cards has grown to 4.6, with half of college students having four or more cards."[6] The same website shows that the average credit card debt for a college student is $3,173, all the while students are accumulating debt with college loans to pay for tuition. The average college debt for loans is close to $30,000, but many students amass much more. I knew of one student who had nearly $20,000 in credit card debt divided over four different cards and over $40,000 in student loans to pay when he left college.

Obviously every case is different, but this incredible amount of credit card debt is mostly related to the fact that we cannot delay gratification. When we see something that catches our eye being advertised, or if we see someone wearing or playing with the latest fad, we want it now. So we buy it. Unfortunately, adaptation takes away our satisfaction shortly after we've tried to fill our restless void with another purchase. "As people come to expect instant gratification in virtually all areas of their lives," writes Brian Seaward, "it creates an undercurrent of anger when the expectations are not met."[7] Anger, frustration, and resentfulness are the results of a culture expecting instant gratification.

From our dilemma of too many choices, our culture of dissatisfaction, and our need for instant gratification, a culture of resentment has developed. "North America today is seething with resentment. How could this not be when the culture of money [choices] is saturated with images of people who have more [culture of dissatisfaction], who do more, who enjoy more [instant gratification]?"[8]

Gratitude Builds a Receptive Heart

A mellow heart is not resentful. The antidote to resentfulness is gratitude, and gratitude helps us open our hearts. Nearly every faith, along with the saints of those faiths, emphasizes gratitude as the underlying principle of the spiritual life. We have already written about gratitude as a means to remember God's abundance in the face of our culture's sense of hoarding and scarcity. But gratitude is so significant, and yet so missing in much of our materialistic lives that it is necessary to keep this reminder before us.

Much of the resentfulness in our culture comes from our sense of entitlement. Gratitude, or receiving everything as a gift, reminds us that we aren't entitled to anything. Everything comes as a gift from God, and we must be grateful to God for everything we have. Thomas Merton wrote, "To be grateful is to recognize the love of God in everything He has given us—and He has given us everything."[9]

Gratitude and Too Many Choices

How does gratitude speak to a culture of too many choices? Gratitude is itself a choice. Most of us think that our personalities dictate whether we are optimists or pessimists, and that optimists tend to be more grateful while pessimists tend to be more resentful. Research done by the positive psychology movement has discovered that this is not necessarily true. Wilkie Au writes, "Fifty percent of happiness has to do with genetics, **10** percent has to do with our intentional activities, and only 10 percent is circumstantial."[10] This leaves a whopping 30 percent open for us to choose how we want to feel. Circumstances only influence 10 percent of our mood in spite of what folk wisdom would lead us to believe. How we choose to deal with these circumstances makes all the difference.

I recently had an MRI done on my knee and listened to the inevitable verdict: surgery. My first instinct was to be resentful. Why did I slip on the ice and tear my meniscus? Why did this have to happen to me? Why do hospitals charge so much, and why do I have to supplement a physician's already bloated salary? The more my thoughts went in this direction, the angrier I became. The irony is that I was working on this very section of this book at the time of my medical diagnosis. I immediately challenged myself to choose to respond gratefully rather than resentfully. "Thank God for surgeons and a medical industry that can repair my knee and help me function without pain," I thought. I am sure that my blood pressure went down considerably after I changed my attitude from resentment to gratitude.

Gratitude and Dissatisfaction

The culture of dissatisfaction seeks to build up one's ego and self-worth by continually accumulating material goods along with exotic experiences. This ego inflation is the opposite of what Jesus calls us to do. He calls us to die to the self, which he himself did better than any other spiritual teacher. "In whatever life circumstance, Jesus always responded with the same motion of self-emptying," writes Cynthia Bourgeault. "Or to put it another way, of the same motions of *descent*: going lower, taking the lower place, not the higher."[11] Instead of trying to grab everything for himself, Jesus gave it all away: ultimately his own life. This self-emptying illustrates the abundance described in chapter 2 and was the essence of Jesus' life. Philip Newell calls this self-giving extravagance love. "Jesus teaches us that we will truly find ourselves only by giving ourselves away in love."[12]

This abundance, generosity, and love are the earmarks of a spacious heart and leave us with an attitude of gratitude. Such a heart in the face of a culture of dissatisfaction comes through generously giving away both your possessions and your self.

Gratitude and Instant Gratification

How does gratitude speak to a culture of instant gratification? The key is to take a longer view. So often we want instant gratification because we are feeling emotionally deprived. The reason could be anything from a severe loss to a trivial hurt from something someone said to us. Jokes abound about women going shopping to fill this "need" for gratification, and men filling it with sex or drink.

A longer view gives us perspective. Henri Nouwen tells us to change our concept of time from *chronos* to *kairos*, two Greek words for time.[13] *Chronos* is clock time, calendar time, while *kairos* is God's time. When we want to make a compulsive purchase, or indulgently consume something unnecessary because of a wounded ego, we are operating on *chronos* time. If instead we would look for what God is wanting to teach us through that "woundedness," our perspective becomes *kairos* time—a God moment.

A good example of these two concepts of time is illustrated in the story of Joseph in the book of Genesis, in the Hebrew Scriptures. In *chronos* time, as the events unfolded by the human calendar, all appeared to be bad. Joseph was an egotistical tattletale whose brothers sold him into slavery. Even though he rose to the top, he was jailed because of a woman's jealousy, and only a few dream interpretations saved his skin. In *kairos* time, however, all of these seemingly bad events worked together to save his family from starvation and to move God's story of deliverance forward. *Kairos* time is the longer view, a view that gives us perspective, not the view of instant gratification.

Julian of Norwich, the great fifteenth century English mystic, wrote, "All will be well, all will be well, and all manner of things will be well." It is thought that she wrote this in order to deal with some sort of painful loss. Whatever the reason she wrote this, it has been quoted through the ages to help people get through crises of all sorts, whether they are personal or national. The saying puts any event in God's time—*kairos* time. I wonder if Joseph had a similar phrase playing in his mind. *Kairos* time keeps our expectations from being immediate. When you have such a perspective, instant answers to perplexing questions are not a concern. We can place our trust in God and in God's time.

When we're able to say "all will be well," we become less anxious, making room in our hearts for spiritual awakening. When we see things from a longer perspective, we can be grateful for the moments when God has broken through in the past and confident that things will work out no matter how difficult they are at the present time.

❧

EXPERIENCING GOD: IN BINDWEED AND FLOWER (SHARON)

My garden nemesis is bindweed—wild morning glory—a noxious weed. Bindweed thrives despite my attempts to eradicate by pulling, digging, spraying with vinegar and soap, or even dousing with boiling water. Nothing stops those persistent vines from curling up the tall stems of other flowers.

Cultivating gratitude and weeding out resentment is similarly labor intensive. The gospel invites us to transform our lives, yet we're seldom taught how that is done. We're instructed to display good character traits, but we aren't shown personal examples of the process of becoming. People hesitate to share because the process is untidy with frequent backtracking. It's easier to close up than be patiently open. Transformation is ongoing, often subtle, and takes time.

Like bindweed, resentment is insidious in my garden of attitudes. Roots of established bindweed plants may extend thirty feet laterally and thirty feet deep. I joke about hitting water from the antipodal Pacific Ocean while digging up roots. Small root pieces left in the ground become new plants. The complicated root system actually nourishes itself once established, so thirty-seven years of pulling out those tenacious roots hasn't done much to clean our property of this weed. It's equally difficult to rid myself of resentment, especially when I want to feel peevish! Then, my most honest prayer is simply asking God to help me want to be grateful.

I'm reminded of the movie *Evan Almighty* when actor Morgan Freeman, acting as God, says, "If someone prays for patience, you think God gives them patience? Or does he give them the opportunity to be patient?" Life offers me countless invitations to turn toward gratitude. While I love God's sense of humor, both as portrayed by Freeman and in my own experience, it takes time to see the humor too.

The vines of my current resentment took root years ago. When I was young I hated the long hours picking peas or mulching potatoes in my dad's garden. Around age twelve, the lure of money had me picking tomatoes on my cousin's farm. Hot sun, flies from the nearby cow pasture biting my arms and legs, and disgust over tomato juice dripping from the chins of other pickers as they ate warm tomatoes cemented a previous vow of never marrying a farmer. Yet all my future husband had to do was bring me to his farm during lambing season and I fell in love with both farm and farmer. The love of raising lambs and watching kittens play wore off quickly in the presence of all the farm work.

Besides the monotonous chores, a good portion of my life revolved around waiting for the farmer to come home. I longed for mental stimulation and summer vacations. The work, animal smells, waiting alone with children, or lying in bed listening for the sound of the planting-cultivating-harvesting equipment returning home took their toll on me. Nourished with powerlessness and ungracious feelings of accusation, boredom, and ingratitude, resentment began to grow. Once fed, resentment grows like the pernicious bindweed that chokes flowers and vegetables in my garden.

While some of my responses to farm life in the past were important clues for personal growth, some became reactionary patterns that etched themselves into daily life. It took years to discern what boundaries I could set around the farm and myself and still have a healthy marriage. Though I often put the farm ahead of my own development, I also found ingenious ways to cope, learning to love farm life. Hardship helped me understand humanity, women's struggles, and how

God, through our everyday life situations and choices, invites us toward self-awareness, consciousness, and transformation. Recently, my husband took an extra job that quickly expanded from part time to overtime. Tendrils of resentment grew as I spent days, evenings, and weekends alone. I questioned why we were revisiting things already processed in our marriage: role expectations, how often one partner is asked to sacrifice, how much work is actually healthy.

During this time there were other stresses. Overwhelmed, I complained to my spiritual director. She asked me a simple question that stunned me. "What and how much can you give without feeling resentful?"

The question evoked the exact opposite of graciousness and openness. I wanted validation or empathy and gave myself guilt instead. I followed her suggestion to dialogue with resentment as a way of opening myself. Perhaps a simple need is not being met; perhaps I'm acting in an old pattern that no longer serves me; perhaps life is asking our marriage relationship to grow. So, I took resentment to my prayer garden, and there on a cozy bench among the lilies, lantana, and bindweed we had a long chat.

I meditated on the quotes in my journal from Joseph Campbell: "Suffering, for me, is whenever we are not in control. It is our opposition to the moment, our inner resistance that says, 'I don't want it to be this way.' The ego is always trying to control reality and therefore it is suffering, because reality is never fully what we want."[14]

Was my resentment a lack of patience and trust that Jay would also discover the best way for us? Was I resentful because I had no control over what was presenting in my life? Was I choosing suffering because it fit old beliefs, a sort of "noble" suffering servanthood, when in truth, I was just not utilizing my power?

For years I kept a daily gratitude journal, yet resentment persisted. I tried to cultivate what Cynthia Bourgeault calls a contemplative attitude: soft, open, and yielding rather than hardened, braced, or resistant.[15] I struggled to hold the tension of all this while gathering wisdom and courage to change.

One night, I woke abruptly. A voice called my name. Clear and urgent, it contained the perfect balance of love and power. I sat up and looked around; Jay was sleeping beside me. In the stillness my soul recognized the voice of love, of wisdom. I felt spacious, not peaceful exactly, but it was enough to lay back and fall asleep instantly.

In the morning, it was easier to ask for gratitude, to trust God would show up however God wanted, rather than expecting I could order what the showing up would look like. Eventually, Jay quit the job. I was humbled, knowing I'd also made choices that didn't benefit both of us.

Though I dislike bindweed, I marvel over the plant's resilience. With God's help, I can be courageous and transform. My greatest power lies in allowing all things, both weeds and cultivated flowers, to teach me a little more about myself, a little more about God.

CHAPTER 5

Invite Your Demons to Tea

.... FEAR OF FLYING (DON)

I was flying in a small plane between the island of Roatan and the coastal city of La Ceiba, Honduras. There were five of us plus luggage packed in the four-seat Cessna aircraft. "I have just enough fuel to reach the coast," said the pilot before takeoff. "So I'm not worried about having one extra passenger aboard." We barely cleared the trees at the end of the runway, but soon we were sailing smoothly above the Caribbean on what seemed like a perfect day. After about fifteen minutes of flying, we ran into a squall that appeared suddenly without warning. The plane started to lose altitude within the squall, and every attempt the pilot made to gain back the lost altitude resulted in the plane stalling and dropping even more. We were buffeted by winds and rain, and the plane was flailing around at the complete mercy of the storm. I was gripped by fear. I was ready to hit the water, and I imagined what would happen to us in the ocean if we survived the crash.

When we finally emerged from the storm, we spotted the shoreline in the distance, but there were no familiar landmarks to identify where we were. We had no idea how far the storm had pushed us off course. Then I remembered the pilot's word that he had just enough fuel to reach the coast. A new worry grabbed me. There were hundreds of miles of undeveloped jungle along the Caribbean coast of Honduras, and even if we were able somehow to land the airplane on a strip of beach, how many days would it take until we would finally be discovered? We had no food or water with us, just several suitcases full of dirty clothes.

We followed the coastline to the west and shortly, the city of our destination, La Ceiba, appeared on the horizon. Although I loved to fly and even took flying lessons for a time, we couldn't land soon enough. When I stepped out of the plane, my legs shook uncontrollably. My colleague's face was ashen as if he had seen a ghost. We both knew that we had barely escaped death, and through our experience, we understood how the emotion of fear can consume a person. We didn't kiss the ground, but gratitude and a profound love for life filtered in where fear had reigned.

ॐ

God is love. Whoever lives in love lives in God, and God in them. There is no fear in love. But perfect love drives out fear, because fear has to do with punishment. The one who fears is not made perfect in love.
—1 JOHN 4:16, 18

Do not be afraid, little flock, for your Father has been pleased to give you the kingdom. Sell your possessions and give to the poor. Provide purses for yourselves that

will not wear out, a treasure in heaven that will never
fail, where no thief comes near and no moth destroys. For
where your treasure is, there your heart will be also.

—LUKE 12:32-34

The Paradox of Trust and Fear

"In God We Trust," proclaim all the bills of the U.S. currency. You'd think that trusting in God would be the end of our fear. The irony of the inscription on our money is that most citizens of the United States, because of fear, appear to put more trust in the dollar bill than in God.

Similarly, a security company in my town posts a huge sign advertising, "Hawk Security Systems." At the very top of the same sign, in letters nearly as large as the name of the business, appears the same motto as on our national currency, "In God We Trust." If we truly trusted in God, would we need security systems? If we didn't fear losing our possessions, would we need alarms?

Fear has always been around. It is part of the human experience. We were created with a certain amount of fear in order to survive. According to Richard Rohr, "'do not be afraid' appears 365 times in the Bible."[1] Because fear can hold us hostage and distract us from trust, we need to be reminded over and over not to be afraid. We need to be reminded of God's provision.

Most of us who call ourselves Christians want to trust in God and God's providence. The motto "In God we trust" and how we use it illustrates the paradox with which most U.S. Americans live. On one hand, we want to believe what our money says. On the other hand, we are afraid to totally trust in God and build larger and supposedly more secure systems of defense.

A Century of Fear

Since the end of World War II, in spite of unprecedented wealth and prosperity, fear has been pandemic in the United

States. Enormous social change during this period, which
made it seem that the world was spinning out of control, is
the root of this fear. It began with fear of the Soviet Union
and the threat of a nuclear attack and continued with the
changes wrought by the civil rights movement of the 1960s.
The Vietnam War, the assassinations of the Kennedy brothers and Martin Luther King Jr., and the peace protests and
hippie movement all added to the angst that everything was
falling apart.

The environmental crisis first received national attention
with Rachel Carson's book *Silent Spring,* and the energy crisis of the late 1970s added fuel to the growing conflagration
of anxiety encompassing the nation. The 1980s brought U.S.
President Reagan's fear mongering with regards to the Soviet
threat in Latin America, propping up in the process some of
the worst dictatorships the civilized world has ever seen.

The optimism of the late 80s and early 90s, when relationships began to thaw with the Soviet Union, apartheid
ended, and the Berlin Wall fell, was replaced by fear through
the events of September 11, 2001. Fear, some of it irratio-
nal, became firmly entrenched in the psyche of every U.S.
American. This irrationality causes us to try to "circle the
wagons" close to home, hoping to relieve the fear with control—often to an extreme. As we will see in chapter 6, boundaries are set for what is right and what is wrong, and these
boundaries are defended, sometimes to the extreme. Black
and white answers are proposed not only to deal with ambiguity, but also to combat fear. Like the paradox of trusting
God while trusting our money, black and white answers only
increase our anxiety about truth, and both increase our fear.

The Media Exacerbates Our Fears

The media brings other horrific national and international
events into the most intimate corners of our homes, adding to
the notion that our world is spiraling out of control. Because
we see these horrors in our homes, the events seem like they
happened right in our own neighborhood. Random school

shootings and other violent crimes, bombings of federal buildings, and mass murders and rape make the headlines. Over-the-counter drugs being tampered with and potential pandemics like H1N1 (swine flu), HIV/AIDS, and E. coli hold the nation in fear.

While much of what is reported is factual, the way the media presents stories tends to sensationalize them, leaving people with the fear that crime is more prevalent than it really is. Barry Glassner dedicates a whole chapter in his book *The Culture of Fear* to describe the exaggerations to which the media succumb to sell a story.[2] Crimes do happen, but because of the ever-present media and talking heads, they seem closer to us and more prevalent than they really are.

Fear of Losing Our Loved Ones

Amid this paranoia—exaggerated or not—and the need for personal control, several generations of children are being raised by a phenomenon called "helicopter parents." These are parents who hover over their children in an attempt to protect them even after they have left home to attend college. "The rise of the helicopter parent corresponds to a rising culture of protectiveness across the board," writes David Kinnaman in his book *You Lost Me*. "Protectiveness has become a way of life in our culture."[3] This overprotectiveness has a direct relationship with the pandemic of fear.

Baby proofing a house for a toddler is another example of this protectiveness. It's a wonder any of us survived our childhood with all the warnings and well-intentioned public service announcements about child safety that parents receive today. We are so focused on protection and avoidance and afraid of what could potentially happen that we forget to provide spaces in our homes that encourage free play and healthy development for our children.

Unfortunately, as much as we would like to protect our kids and isolate them from the media-exaggerated horrors of the real world, we cannot. The university where I work requires a cross-cultural experience as part of its general education program. My wife and I have led several semester-long programs to Guatemala and Mexico. Parents are always concerned, and rightly so, about the safety of their children while they are in the program. Because of all the national attention on the drug wars in Mexico and the ensuing violence, they are especially concerned when we go there, even though the city where our program is located has the lowest crime rate in all of Mexico. Nevertheless, despite my trying to assuage their fears with websites detailing crime rates and the relative safety of the city, I always receive several concerned emails from parents before we leave.

One year I received a particularly anxious email from two parents. I doubt that I was ever able to alleviate all their anxiety with my response, but I tried. Interestingly, just four days before we were going to return to the United States, we received word of the shootings that had occurred at Virginia Tech in April of 2007. As details of the shooting became available, we learned that the perpetrator was a high school classmate of the student in our group whose parents held the most concern for her safety. No matter how concerned or protective one is, there is no way to protect anyone from random acts of violence. Being overprotective or "hovering" only adds to the fear and debilitating anxiety.

Fear of Losing Our Lifestyle

Another source of fear is worry over the loss of our lifestyle, a lifestyle in which we have amassed more "stuff" than any other society in history. My home, which was built in the 1950s, has a one-car garage that barely allows room for a car. Few homes are built today with less than a two-car garage, with huge amounts of space not only for our humongous vehicles, but also space to store all the "needs" we have accumulated. For many, a spacious two-car garage is not enough, so little garden sheds are built in our backyards to store more of our necessities. If that is not enough, the storage industry in the United States is expanding rapidly so that U.S. Americans have more room to store their junk.

As outlined in the chapter on gratitude and resentfulness, this accumulation of worldly goods does not bring about satisfaction or happiness. But beyond the lack of satisfaction, having so much makes us inordinately fearful of losing what we have—both as individuals and as a nation.

The United States spends nearly as much on its military budget as all the rest of the world combined.[4] The rhetoric given for such expenditures is to "keep the world safe for democracy" and to "protect our freedom." The reality is that it is to protect the consumptive lifestyle we are accustomed to. And losing that lifestyle creates fear. "When we feel entitled to what we have, we resent any threat to our possessions, yet when we fear losing the objects of our misplaced desire, we really fear God working in our lives."[5] Our things are our identity. We trust in them more than we trust in God in spite of what our money says. If only we could understand that security doesn't come from more preparedness for war. True security (absence of fear) and freedom (an open heart) begin from within us.

Anthony de Mello claims that fear is the root of all other maladies in our culture, if not in all cultures. "[T]here's not a single evil in the world that you cannot trace to fear," he writes. "Not one."[6] For de Mello, anger and violence are caused by fear: fear of having something taken from us. "Think of the last time you were angry," he continues, "and search for the fear behind it. What were you afraid of losing? That's where the anger comes from."[7] So according to this logic, if we are afraid of losing what we have—and indeed we have so much to lose—we must be a very angry people.

"In God we trust." Do we indeed?

Perfect Love Drives Out Fear

How do we swim against the stream in the face of such constant pressure to be fearful? The most basic answer to this question is to really live that which is stamped on U.S. money. Trust in God instead of our possessions; trust in God instead of our bank accounts, retirement funds, or insurance policies.

Trust in God instead of our bloated military and our home security systems. "Do not be afraid!" Trust in God by following Jesus' teaching on love.

When Jesus was asked by a Jewish lawyer what he needed to do in order to inherit eternal life, he answered: "You shall love the Lord your God with all your heart, and with all your soul, and with all your strength, and with all your mind; and your neighbor as yourself" (Luke 10:27). In Matthew 22:40, he adds, "On these two commandments hang all the law and the prophets." I would add that on these two commandments hang all the considerations of spirituality. On these two commandments hang the love that drives out fear. On these two commandments hang our spacious hearts.

"Perfect love drives out fear," writes John in his first epistle. "There is no fear in love" (1 John 4:16). If we trust completely in God and love him with all our "heart, soul, strength and mind," we will find that our fear will dissipate. This is the answer to combating our compulsive acquisitiveness and hoarding. To have "treasure in heaven that will never fail" instead of temporal treasures that a thief can steal and a moth can destroy, we need the spiritual disciplines, the first of which is detachment. The ability to let God be in charge and the ability to be detached from material possessions is found in all the writings of the saints and sages throughout the ages.

Perfect Love Means Love Your Neighbor

"And [love] your neighbor as yourself." The lawyer wanted to know who his neighbor was, and Jesus follows with the story of the good Samaritan in Luke 20. The neighbor is not only someone you live beside and get along with well, but is also, in the case of Jesus' story, the hated mixed-race, unclean Samaritan. For us a neighbor may be the one who causes undue fear whenever you think about him or her, or the one who lives on the margins of our society and is considered a "poor soul," or who is looked at as an enemy.

Jesus repeats this sentiment in nearly all of his teaching. "Love your enemies," he says. "Do good to those who hate you, and pray for those who insult you and persecute you" (Matthew 5:44). This kind of love transcends the national boundaries that have historically created such unmerited fear. Most of these boundaries have been arbitrarily set by politicians and not by God. Difficult as it may be, loving our enemies is perfect love—love that casts out fear. It is loving your neighbor as yourself. This is the mind of Christ.

We have been so culturally conditioned to think in terms of nation states, enemies, and threats that we have lost Jesus' vision of perfect love and loving our neighbor as ourselves. Putting into practice the perfect love that Jesus talked about is difficult but important. Even loving our friends and family is not as easy as it should be and comes with a certain cost. How much more difficult is it to extend that love to the unlovely neighbor, the alien, the enemy, and those who live across boundaries we set up? We desire love for those close to us. Can this desire be applied to relationships beyond our familiar circles?

To be truly Christian—followers of the teachings of Christ—the answer to this question is yes. If more Christians would identify with the kingdom of God instead of the kingdom of the United States, or the United Kingdom, or the kingdom of Honduras, or whatever earthly kingdom, the answer is yes. To be truly mellow of heart and to conquer our fear, the answer is also yes.

Experiencing God's Perfect Love through Quieting Our Souls
Most of the fears outlined in this chapter could be quelled by quieting ourselves before God and allowing his perfect love to flow into our souls. This is a spiritual discipline championed over the years by all the spiritual giants of nearly every religion. Too few of us have the patience or take the time to be still before God because we are afraid of what we might find out about ourselves—even our fears. But this quiet time with God brings us a more spacious heart, a heart that has room for spiritual awakening.

ટ⚫

EXPERIENCING GOD: BEFRIENDING FEAR (SHARON)

My words are small.
And expansive
as the canyon lands in Utah.

My words are often unspoken,
silent and succulent,
a desert both muted and
wildly alive.
My words are powerful.
They cut me open.
They bathe me
in warm hugs.

I am small.
As microscopic life teeming
in the desert floor,
rich lichen on rock.

My words widen me,
open me, expand me,
until I am the child discovering
lichen green
on stones,
the woman standing
surrounded by mountain peaks
she's climbed,

the artist hammering
metal, the moon
slivered in a sky, the spider web
cradling dew, throwing sunlight
all around.

Feeling small is probably not unique to me. At some point in our lives, when we encounter greatness or stand next to riveting beauty, incredible talent, or experience an awesome God, we just feel small. Often we are afraid. We doubt our own beauty, worth, or relevance. We fear our inadequacies, our limitations, our appetites and desires; we even fear our capacity for intimacy, transparency, and deep loving. We are so determined to be courageous and Christian that we find ourselves battling, denying, or running away from our fears without realizing those methods mean we are still focusing on them, thus giving them energy.

A wise friend once told me the secret to dealing with fear is "to sit down at the table and invite your demons to tea." Whatever monster you constantly fight or run from often gets bigger and more menacing, so inviting the monster to your house for tea means putting down your guilt, your determination to eradicate it; instead, befriend, welcome, and get to know what parts of yourself are inflating or creating the monster. I remember my initial reaction of simultaneous repulsion and attraction to this invitation. Is it even possible to open myself enough to invite my demons to tea? Invite my fears, worries, shortcomings—all the things I hide from myself and others—and stay with them long enough to see, acknowledge, and make peace over a cup of tea? Maybe one at a time, and over many cups!

Pouring tea and sharing a cup with someone means you face the other—know their name. I may or may not like this tablemate, may not agree or want to encourage whatever he, she, or it represents, but I am awake, aware, and acknowledging their presence. While communing over tea there is no battle or escape; there is only humility, integrity, wisdom, and self-awareness. And when I also mindfully invite Divine Love to the table, interesting things happen. Love invited brings healing and transformation. There is courage and calm in the presence of fear. If not courage and calm immediately, then at least a tiny space opens up between the fear arising and the fanning of that fear or acting unconsciously because of it.

Freedom to "not be afraid" lies in developing that space and then choosing your reactions.

What does living courageously look like? I'll begin by stating some of my own wrestling with life's difficulties and the suffering that causes us fear in the first place. Nothing completely protects us from storms, illness, broken bones, and accidents. There is a lot of positive thinking around telling us what we believe affects our destinies; what we affirm we attract. The postmodern "law of attraction" movement is valuable. We do have more power to change our lives than we realize. I am very grateful for what this movement is bringing to our awareness. I've learned these truths in a thousand tiny ways: when I worry about not finding a parking space, I often can't find one. When I relax and trust the process of finding a parking space, I usually find one fairly easily. Perhaps the often-debunked prayer for a parking space is simply this "law" in effect . . . by focusing on what you want or on a loving trustworthy God rather than on fear, a space to park can be seen more easily. Yet, I can also see the limitations of positive thinking, affirming, and attracting. No matter how good we are at being optimistic, at attracting what we desire, no matter if we become geniuses at understanding the human body, psychology, and transformation, there are always possibilities of rogue storms and destruction of our wealth and health.

Yes, we all have a soul, a holy imprint, a Divine spark in us, whatever we call it. We can experience oneness with creation and with God, but we are not God. Even tending to our interior work, becoming open, self-aware, thinking positively, and healing and affirming our lives is no guarantee that life is not going to be difficult. A traditional approach of "name it and claim it" or a postmodern "law of attraction," or any kind of prosperity gospel tends to leave out other persons' or other groups' realities; we can't control or manipulate the interiors of others. Not all of us transform at the same rate; other people's interiors and reactions will affect our world. We also can't control all aspects of earth, nature, and the cosmos. When a tsunami hits, we do not personally attract it. Earthquakes or weather patterns cause tsunamis, and perhaps our collective contribution to global warming as well.

When Hurricane Sandy moved up the northeast coast in 2012, media prepared folks for a "Frankenstorm." Jay and I responded differently to the threat. I wanted to do everything possible to prepare; Jay was all "wait and see." He's not inclined to batten down anything until strong wind motivates him.

I've watched him calmly gather eggs in our chicken house while the western sky bunched up blackness against light like a sinister quilt. When our radio belched tornado warnings, his calloused hands never broke their rhythm. He usually leaves the field at the last minute to put away equipment or close wildly flapping barn doors that I can't struggle to close on my own.

As Sandy approached, I watched the news and relayed information to Jay, as he was furiously harvesting corn before the damaging winds could blow stalks down. Filling jugs of water, worrying about not having a generator, and fighting fear (storms tend to make me forget the fear-tea ceremony), I grouched about our differences. Jay harvested nonstop to save the corn and our income; I pleaded with him to stop just long enough to buy a generator and protect our food supply. Not being heard increased my anxiety.

In the midst of fretting, I needed to quiet my mind, open my heart, and center myself in trust and love. In my meditation room, soft afternoon light shone through the window. There, I was surrounded by reminders of love: a red feather given as a sign of hope during cancer, the rock with a wire-sculpted climber showing perseverance in the face of difficulty, and the large Peruvian Momma figurine hugging a child—my reminder of Divine Love.

Pine boughs swayed outside, birds fed hungrily before the storm. Stillness seeped into my body as I felt my steady heartbeats. From the calm a question arose: Will you trust even when there is no reassurance?

I was being asked to choose between fear and trust, between control and surrender. I wanted to close my heart to this question, and then I realized my annoyance felt more in control than my fear. Such insight prepared me to welcome anger and fear. *God, I'm scared! Is that such an inappropriate response?* I sensed God's answering smile. Of course not, but fanning fear and allowing indignation to cover or validate it doesn't open you to trust.

The red maple on the front lawn glowed outside my window. Yellow finches clung to swinging seed feeders. Suddenly, the world seemed safe; I breathed deeply, noticing the easier flow of my thoughts: *Even if trees fall, new ones grow. Lives may be lost—even mine—but winter will come after autumn and spring after winter. Life is not without difficulty. Storms and fears will arise, but love carries me. This house is old, but strongly built. There may be damages, but we are resilient. We may lose our store of food, but starvation is most likely not going to happen.*

With a more spacious heart, I had room for all that was presenting. I don't like feeling overwhelmed by forces of nature, controlling people, or strong emotions. Especially when I feel small. My open heart found wisdom for understanding myself and God a little more. God has my back. This knowledge wasn't a guarantee of protection from harm, but reassurance of interior calm and strength. Like the moon vision in the introduction to this book, I felt Love's embrace in the midst of this storm. Fear was present, but I could witness it from the sidelines. All was well with my soul.

CHAPTER 6

What If She Is a Crazy Mystic and Levitates or Something?

WATCH THE RIGHT OR WRONG (DON)

Most of us think that the biblical commandment "Thou shalt not steal" (Exodus 20:15) is pretty clear. But what we consider to be personal property to be stolen is culturally defined. I shared a room with a Honduran man while doing development work for a mission agency in La Ceiba, Honduras. I had two watches. I left one on top of the common dresser in our room while I wore the other one. One day I noticed the watch on the dresser had gone missing and spied it on my Honduran roommate's arm. I was furious, wondering how he dare "steal" my watch and be so bold as to wear it in my presence.

I tried to approach him without being too accusatory, but I'm sure he could sense my frustration. What I didn't know was that Hondurans, being a collectivistic culture, see anything within the same room as something that can be shared by all within the same room. What was his was also mine. My culture, being individualistic, divides everything in the room between "his" and "mine." So what I thought was stealing, he considered to be communal property for the residents of the same room. He never thought he was stealing. He didn't understand the difference between our views of personal, private property.

After my accusations, what he used to justify his use of my watch caught me up short. He told me that he was helping me be a better steward of my property because the watch's potential was going unused lying there on the dresser. By his comment, the vast difference between our worldviews was underscored. The way each of us approached personal property and its use or lack of use makes the seemingly black and white commandment somewhat fuzzy. Did he steal? Was I a poor steward of my possessions? The one thing we had in common was that we were both followers of Jesus and took the Ten Commandments seriously. What made the watch incident ambiguous was how our socialization regarding the meaning of private property differed. To grow a more spacious heart we need to understand our ambiguous time and learn to deal with it.

ès

For my yoke is easy and my burden is light. —Matthew 11:30

Now we see only a dim likeness of things. It is as if we were seeing them in a mirror. But someday we will see clearly. We will see face to face. What I know now is not complete. But someday I will know completely, just as God knows me completely. —1 Corinthians 13:12 (NIRV)

Baseball Rules

I love the game of baseball. I have played it, and no matter where I have lived, I have followed the team of my boyhood for over fifty years. But just try to imagine playing baseball, or any sport for that matter, without any rules. It would be chaos. Major League Baseball has a book governing the game that is 176 pages long. It is updated every year as rules evolve to reflect current realities.

Like the rules for the game of baseball, every society makes a social contract to control the behavior of its citizens; many of them are written in books of law that are interpreted by lawyers and judges in the courts. Many cultural understandings of how to live together are unwritten codes that one grows up learning and incorporating into one's behavior. Businesses, schools, religions, and every other organization sets up rules for its governance. Everyone wants to know "how to play the game."

When the rules are not clear, or are ambiguous, we become disoriented and confused. I remember a baseball game played at the old Houston Astrodome. A ball was hit so hard that it caromed off a speaker at the very pinnacle of the domed roof. The ball clearly would have been a home run in any other stadium in the country, but it hit that speaker and came back into the field of play, causing much confusion because the ground rules for the park didn't cover the very unlikely possibility of a ball hitting a speaker on the ceiling. The umpires decided that the ball should still be in play when it came down on the field, so one of the longest balls ever hit in the history of the park became a single. You can imagine the chaos caused by the ambiguity of the rule. One side was elated while the other was irate. Arguments ensued and it took several minutes for peace to be restored in order for the game to continue.

Ambiguous Times

Like the confusion caused by the unclear rule and change in environment at a baseball game, we live in a time that is defined by ambiguity. Many of the rules of the game that were once assumed to be immutable are changing, and some of them are changing at breakneck speed. Increased travel, the Internet, more emigration, and newscasts from every corner of the globe have brought the remotest idea from the farthest point on the globe right into our homes and neighborhoods. Where once it took years for the revolutionary ideas of Frenchman Voltaire to reach the shores of North and South America to influence their political thinking, today's information is instantaneous. Our worldview is constantly being challenged by other ways of thinking and being.

Nowhere has this been more evident than in religion and spirituality. What was once understood as a basic Judeo-Christian culture in North America has become a mosaic of religions and cultures. During the chaos of the 1960s, many influential people turned to Eastern religions for enlightenment and a so-called New Age spirituality began to emerge—one that didn't adhere to any organized religion and borrowed from any and all religions. After the attack on the World Trade Center towers on September 11, 2001, the need to understand Islam and the Muslim world came to the forefront in many circles, including the university where I teach. Centers for interfaith dialogue began cropping up everywhere.

Because of increased dialogue with other faiths, Christians, especially younger ones, are questioning Jesus' claim "I am the way and the truth and the life, no one comes to the father except through me" (John 14:6). What is truth, and which religion holds the key to the truth? Isn't there truth in all religions? How can God condemn people to hell who have never heard of Jesus? These are questions I hear nearly every day in teaching young adults. What used to be clear rules for how to play the religious game have now become ambiguous and many people have become disoriented and confused.

There are some absolute truths that all peoples can agree on, you can protest, like the Ten Commandments. Nearly all religions have a similar list of "thou shalt nots." The watch incident that I recounted earlier from my cross-cultural experience shows that even these nearly absolute truths are interpreted differently from culture to culture.

When everyone in the room agrees on how to define private property, it is clear what stealing is. When there are differing definitions about private property in the same room, what stealing means becomes ambiguous. Take that little incident between two people and expand it to understand what is happening in our neighborhood, our country, and our world. In 2008, 41 percent of the public school students in Harrisonburg, Virginia, where I live, were non-native speakers of English. Although three-quarters of these students had Spanish as their primary language, there were forty-nine other language groups represented.[1] I wonder how many different definitions of private property are represented among such a diverse group of students.

Can't Deal with Ambiguity. Give Me Some Rules.

In order to deal with this ambiguity, people groups, and especially religious groups, set up strict rules to define who is *in* and who is *out*. For example, the church that I grew up in applied a strict set of rules to govern the behavior of their members in order to combat the threat of modernism in theology on the one hand, and the increasing suburbanization of its population and the accompanying temptations to worldliness, on the other hand. These situations caused ambiguity and disorientation. The rules were an attempt to make what was unclear be more sharply defined, hopefully providing some orientation. The rules governed dress and lifestyle issues ranging from the prohibition of musical instruments to radios and television. Bishops, many who were feared, were installed to keep members of the church in line.

Like the church of my boyhood, history is replete with churches and religious groups that get caught up in setting rules to govern behavior and to lessen ambiguity. Adhering strictly to a set of rules is called legalism. According to

Charles Smoot, "Legalism is a belief system where [one] gets merit through keeping laws or [human]-made doctrines, disciplines, or rules to obtain righteousness with God as well as favor, blessings, and the promise of eternal life for him or herself."[2]

As a sectarian Christian group back then, my church certainly thought that they were securing favor and eternal life for themselves by following their strict rules. They had a clear sense of what was right and wrong; there was nothing ambiguous. Unfortunately, rules are used to control rather than to liberate. Supposed liberty from ambiguity brought slavery to the rules and an emphasis on outer rather than inner spirituality. Fortunately, I believe that the church of my youth has mostly moved beyond rules and regulations and has become interested in an authentic spirituality. That is what this book is about.

Legalism Not Jesus' Way!

Indeed, Jesus' main criticism of the Pharisees in the New Testament was about the superficiality of their rules and regulations. Matthew 23 is a litany of woes and strong language against the Pharisees and teachers of the law for their legalism. "They tie up heavy, cumbersome loads and put them on other people's shoulders, but they themselves are not willing to lift a finger to move them," and "You travel over land and sea to win a single convert, and when you have succeeded, you make them twice as much a child of hell as you are" (Matthew 23:4, 15). The implication is that for a person to become a Jew, they had to be saddled with all the regulations of the religion, most of which were external. This not only made the burden too heavy to carry, but also put the converts in a situation that did not really guarantee their salvation.

Both-And Thinking

Like the Pharisees in Jesus' time and my experience in my boyhood church, too many people deal with ambiguity through rules, regulations, and either/or, black-and-white thinking. Developing a mellow heart and a healthy spirituality makes it necessary for us to move beyond this simplistic way of viewing the world. Richard Rohr writes, "Mature people are not either/or thinkers, but they bathe in the ocean of both-and."[3] Probably most of the tension in political or religious circles revolves around two entrenched views that are at polar opposites. Each side becomes more fixed in its position and defends it.

I was once talking to a fellow Christian service worker at a meeting of evangelical missionaries in Guadalajara, Mexico. We were discussing the fact that I was with an agency that worked in development rather than specifically in evangelism. I also stated that I was often uncomfortable being called a missionary because of the negative stereotypes that abounded about missionaries. Another fellow missionary overheard our conversation and interjected, "You are either a missionary or a mission field." Although I appreciated the pithiness of his comment, I have come to believe that we are all both a missionary *and* a mission field. We all have areas in our lives that need repentance, and at the same time, we are all witnesses of the good news either by what we do or by what we say. The either/or thinking leads to tension in the nerves and knots in the stomach. Either/or thinking does not lead to an open, tender heart.

Either/Or Politics

In the political arena in the United States, in a simplistic view, one side wants less government control in people's lives, while the other wants more. Why does it have to be either/or? Why can't there be both government control *and* freedom from government control? We affirm the freedom that capitalism brings to entrepreneurial and hardworking people, but we have also seen the devastation of the unbridled greed of banks during the economic crisis of 2008. Why can't there be both freedom for developing new ideas with appropriate financial rewards *and* some control to allow for checks and balances?

Either/Or Religion

Even our view of God reflects this either/or thinking. The God I grew up with was a strict, angry, authoritarian God who wanted nothing more than to catch me in my sin and strike his judgment against me just like Sodom and Gomorrah. This image was reinforced by the authority figures in my life: the bishop, some relatives, and my father. This image was further reinforced by waves of fervent revival meetings that hit my community in the 1950s and 1960s. I was sure I was going to hell and marched down the sawdust path numerous times to be redeemed of my sins. I feared God as much as I feared the frowning bishop and stern relatives.

This image of God had been the prevailing image of our culture—not just in the church of my boyhood. Henri Nouwen, in his book *The Return of the Prodigal Son*, talks about his own socialized view of a stern, judgmental God. "It dawned on me that even my best theological and spiritual formation had not been able to completely free me from a Father God who remained somewhat threatening and somewhat fearsome," he wrote. "I have seen how the fear of becoming subject to God's revenge and punishment has paralyzed the mental and emotional lives of many people, independently of their age, religion or life-style."[4] This is still the image of God that many evangelical groups carry. Of course, like the story of the destruction of Sodom and Gomorrah, there is biblical evidence for this kind of God.

At some point, perhaps as a reaction to this unbalanced view of God, the emphasis on an all-loving God began to emerge. This view is best reflected in the story of the prodigal son recounted in Luke 15:11-32. Again we return to Nouwen for contrasting this opposing image of God: "God's vision is not that of a stereotypical landowner or patriarch, but rather that of an all-giving and forgiving father who does not measure out his love to his children according to how well they behave."[5] This "all-giving and forgiving father" image of God is prevalent in the writing of most writers on spirituality today as well as in many so-called mainline churches, and is the polar opposite of the God of wrath and judgment. Like the story of the prodigal son, there is also biblical evidence for this image of God.

Because of our need to define things in black and white terms to overcome the ambiguity we face, there is a tendency for some groups to emphasize the God of wrath and others to emphasize the God of love with no middle ground. Since there is scriptural evidence of both a God of wrath and a God of love, shouldn't our view be both-and rather than either/or?

Jesus' Burden Is Light

Having an open heart begins with lightening the load of rules and regulations and either/or thinking. What a contrast between the burdens the Pharisees put on their followers *and* the rules and regulations of the church of my youth and Christ's claim that "my yoke is easy and my burden is light" (Matthew 11:30).

The family of my maternal grandmother showed mellowness of heart in the face of the strict discipline of the church. They enjoyed life to the fullest. To be sure, they followed the rules, but didn't let them overtake their lives. Music, food, and laughter filled our times together—especially laughter. Never-ending stories stretched to ridiculousness—jokes from our Swiss-German ethnic background, some even a bit bawdy, filled the house or yard with laughter and merriment.

When we gathered for family reunions, there was an unbelievable spread of food. Using the traditional Pennsylvania Dutch fare of seven sweets and seven sours as a guide, we gorged ourselves with two meats, mashed potatoes and noodles, and two vegetables. Dessert consisted of two cakes, gelatin, two puddings, and two pies. The indulgence in food made up for the austerity of the church discipline.

What a contrast between the frowns of disapproval from the legalistic enforcers of the burdens of my boyhood church and the peals of laughter of my more rowdy relatives. Their mellow hearts made the "yoke" easier and the "burden" lighter. I think this was Jesus' approach to the Law of his day as well when he said in Mark 2:27: "The Sabbath was made to serve us; we weren't made to serve the Sabbath" (*The Message*). These are also good examples of both-and thinking. "I can both obey the church rules, *and* have a good time," I can imagine my mother's relatives saying. "I can both obey the Sabbath laws *and* relax them when they become too much of a burden." This is the way I imagine Jesus thinking.

Legalism and either/or thinking lead to authoritarianism and conflict. Both-and thinking leads to an open, spacious heart and peace. Both-and thinking helps us to deal with ambiguity. As much as we would like it to be otherwise, life is not like a baseball game that can be regulated with specific, absolute rules. Yes, we need guidelines to live by to prevent anarchy, but as we've seen in the cross-cultural watch-stealing incident, our guidelines are not absolute. We need to live with the tension of some ambiguity.

Is Jesus the Way?

Is Jesus the way the truth and the life? A U.S. Jewish rabbi was once asked this question. "The rabbi replied, 'Oh, I agree with these words.' To which the surprised questioner asked further, 'But how can you as a rabbi believe that Jesus is the way, the truth and the life?' 'Because,' answered the rabbi, 'I believe that Jesus' way is the way of love, that Jesus' truth is the truth of love, and that Jesus' life is the life of love. No one comes to the Father but through love.'"[6]

What a wonderfully astute answer that avoids the black and white, either you are Christian or you are a Jew type of thinking. In our ambiguous age, we need to think more like the Jewish rabbi. We already believe that God has revealed himself to both Jewish people and to Christians. We don't have to give up our faith in Jesus to recognize that God has also revealed himself in special ways to other religions. By holding these disparate beliefs in tension, we are dealing with ambiguity and developing a mellow heart.

Pope John XXIII summed up dealing with ambiguity this way: "In essentials unity, in nonessentials liberty, and in all things, charity."[7] Here we have both unity and freedom, not either unity or freedom. We can agree to disagree on the nonessentials. Deciding what is essential and what is not may cause ambiguity, so we need the third part of his quote, "in all things charity." How far would a dose of charity go in making "rough places plain" (Isaiah 40:4) in not only our religious and political views, but also in our everyday relationships?

My rowdy relatives added a bit of charity to the strict discipline of their church. Jesus added a bit of charity to the Jewish law by offering an easy yoke and a light burden. We could add a bit of charity to everything if we would keep in mind the verse from 1 Corinthians 13:12: "Now we see only a dim likeness of things. It is as if we were seeing them in a mirror. But someday we will see clearly" (NIRV).

૨&

EXPERIENCING GOD: YOKED WITH A MELLOWER GOD (SHARON)

During difficult times in my life, I instinctively devote larger blocks of time for solitude, reflection, and prayer. Recovering from stage four lymphoma and months of chemotherapy was one of those times. Illness has a way of inviting deeper reflection; especially about what is life giving and what is not.

One morning, while praying and meditating on my life and health, a strong visual impression of Jesus standing between two yokes came to mind. One yoke is large and heavy, the other smooth and lighter. Jesus is smiling deeply as he motions to both yokes. I'm drawn to his smile as well as to the options he offers.

"The choice is yours," he invites. "Whatever you choose, I'll love you the same and I'll pull with you." I remember the New Testament verse where Jesus speaks "my yoke is easy and my burden is light" (Matthew 11:30). My dreamlike version is different than how I've internalized this passage in the past. Jesus offers a choice of two yokes. He knows and loves me intimately, and he is light-hearted about my choice. I'm intrigued with this total freedom and deep love.

In my youth and childhood, I mostly encountered a suffering, bloody, shame, and guilt-producing Jesus. I never imagined Jesus laughing, or smiling with twinkling eyes. Well into adulthood, I feared such yoked bondage and didn't believe Jesus' proclamation of lightness and ease.

I'm grateful for my spiritual practices, as they allow me to grow in my experiences of God. Now, I trust the process of the Holy Spirit stirring within me, the bubbling up of images and emotions from my subconscious as a result of my openness in prayer. This process brings me toward greater wholeness. Such grounding in practice increases my trust, moves me out of my head and from debating whether or not this was from God, and into the heart of the vision—allowing myself to be surprised by a new experience of Jesus.

Then, I open to all the questions. Why is Jesus inviting me to decide between a heavy yoke and a light yoke? Are both of these yokes mine, are both his, or is one mine and one his? Why would I choose the heavy, rough one if I had a choice? What if I don't have to be fearful or controlled to be yoked to Jesus? What if I believed it really is up to me to choose what yokes I want to put on? What would it be like partnering with God, co-creating, and pulling side by side through life? What if I keep choosing the heavy yoke, because it's an ingrained, unhealthy pattern of self-sacrificing? Would Jesus keep pulling with me? Does Jesus pulling with me mean I'm super powerful or that I'd be partnering with the One who lovingly assists me while continuing to lead me toward wisdom and self-awareness?

I held this visual impression within me for days, and pondered the questions with mind and heart. I watched Amish farmers in the fields working mules and horses, imagined the yokes, the feel of pulling together. I sometimes prayed with warmed lavender-scented neck pillows draped over my shoulders. I felt the weight, and asked God and my own heart to reveal the meaning of the visual. I told my spiritual director about it and together we explored my thoughts and emotions, always asking what God may be up to in this invitation.

Slowly, I realized I was being invited to replace my old, almost unconscious image of Jesus—the image of one who drives me from behind, or is ahead dragging me along. This old image reminds me of a phrase from a religious song called "Hornet Persuasion." As a child, I listened to this phrase with fear and fascination: "God does not compel us to go 'gainst our will, but He just makes us willing to go." In my childish misconceptions, God was an authoritarian trickster. Sooner or later God would force me with the likes of hornets and earthquakes to do what God wanted; my desires were inconsequential. What a blessing to be invited to know a God who truly wants me to be and do what God put in me at birth to be and do!

God is my partner; we work together to uncover what is in my heart and what my purpose is. The stick that drives me is often some type of cultural conditioning, previous misconception, or a ghost from the authoritarian, black and white religious teachings of my childhood. The image of God as my partner is mellower than my childhood God-images, and opens my heart to a more spacious, generous God. The uncovering of who I am at my truest, deepest level and what I am meant to be and do is a fascinating journey of discovery. There is no tricking or overpowering involved. God desires this for me and draws me with laughter, love, respect, and freedom into self-awareness, ongoing discernment about what gives my life meaning, and the wisdom to know how to best give back in gratitude. When God offers a new image, it is so beautiful and healing, it's easy to replace the old one.

Experiencing God: Holding the Mysteries of the Universe

It is difficult to hold paradoxes, to dwell in questions and the mysteries of the universe without wanting to wear our God theologies like a bulletproof vest or slap a box of answers and rules over confused people, ourselves included. Anyone can awaken to the mystery, to the seeker's journey, and everyone is loved equally whether or not they risk climbing out of their comfort zones. As a spiritual director, I listen to many stories of peoples' journeys through confusion, doubt, and questions, and I witness their experience of freedom after letting go of absolutes. The following story is a good example of this.

"I pretty much believe everyone is going to heaven."

As Kyle blurts out this statement he strokes his goatee nervously, watching me closely, looking for some sign of shock or rejection from me. I am far from shocked; my face remains placid and open, inviting more conversation. I smile to myself at his courage, at the seed of doubt tucked away in his otherwise confident statement. His comment is typical of people in their late twenties, though in my practice I find young and old alike hesitate to make their first ambiguous statements or to question black and white thinking. Every time someone steps close to the edge of their previous plateau of beliefs and dares to question or make unpopular statements to a perceived authority figure, it usually feels risky.

I'm sleepy and tired after setting up the visuals for a silent retreat, meeting all the retreatants, and unpacking my own things. The potato chips I just ate in the snack room of this retreat house are sending their carb-calming signals into my system. I would love to go to my room and collapse, but the hunger for dialogue in his eyes moves me. It is midnight at the Jesuit Center; most retreatants are curled in their beds, sound asleep, enjoying blissful respite from the hubbub of usual life. A few are up and agitated, wrestling with themselves, with God, with deep questions. Some, like Kyle, are nowhere near sleep. They are crackling with aliveness, deeply in love with both the questions and all that is supposedly known, longing for soul friends, community, and conversation.

I've been all of the above at various times in my life. Lately, it seems, every cell in my body vibrates with energy when in the presence of a genuine seeker. Kyle intuits this, I'm sure, and not only sits down to join me, but also begins talking openly despite not having met each other before this moment. We are connected only by our love for this Spirit-breathed place and the nametags proclaiming we are facilitator and student at Kairos: School of Spiritual Formation.

After a few minutes of greeting, followed by some contemplative silence, the young man across the table from me leans forward eagerly. Smiling, I settle back into my chair and rally myself for a late night. I ask him how he came to that statement. He erupts with stories and experiences, telling me of various books he's read, different churches and seminary classes he's been to, and of dialogues he's had with people.

"This is a game changer for you, right?"

Kyle's forehead crinkles in thought. He twirls a plastic daisy from the centerpiece between the thumb and forefinger of his left hand, props his chin on his right. "Well, it frees me to explore a different spiritual terrain. It expands me, brings up thousands of other questions, and asks me to hold the tension of gray area. It is much easier to believe in black and white. In the middle of gray, I don't know anything for sure anymore—that is freeing and frightening at the same time. I don't want to appear apathetic or lacking in confidence, but I've lost some of my religious arrogance. What worries me most is how this exploration separates me from half my relatives. They fear for me."

Ah yes, the relatives. And the church, the school, the ethnic and social groups that form our containers of rules, thoughts, and conditionings much needed for our development—but which are like bassinets that grow tight and need to be crawled out of in order to explore the wild and raw life beyond.

He talks about loneliness, fear, difficulties, and a strong desire for authenticity, transparency, and intimacy, not romance—everyone goes there when I mention intimacy—but real relationships with trusted individuals and community. I listen, enthralled, shivery prickles cascading up and down my arms. He falls silent. Our eyes meet, and we smile, knowing our souls have found deep resonance.

"You may be describing the church and small groups of the future," I say, finally. I wish he could see his glowing face. I'm fairly sure he sees mine. "Our longing is a prayer." I'm speaking to both of us. "Let's keep it alive! Let's keep looking for those who are ready for growth, accountability, and depth, for those who desire emotional health, integration of body, mind, and soul. Imagine the possibilities if enough of us pray and seek."

"It might get worse before it gets better." He looks down, studying the daisy pattern on the plastic tablecloth. He is wise beyond his years.

"Yes, equilibrium follows periods of disequilibrium." Then I tell him about my own first wobbly explorations into all the gray areas, and leaving either/or thinking.

I describe coming to Kairos: School of Spiritual Formation, in my early fifties, as a first-year student. I feel like a kindergartener walking the steps of a huge building. My intuition tells me I will not be the same. Change is brewing. My husband drops me off at the front entrance of the Jesuit Center in Wernersville, the host facility for Kairos, hugs me goodbye, and drives away. I stand there, all alone, staring at wide steps, arches, and marble pillars beckoning the way toward dark polished wooden double doors. What am I really going to experience upon entering those doors? The marked difference in the enormous building before me and the small, plain dwellings of house and church of my childhood feel symbolic of a major transition. Such beauty seems decadent, coming from my simple Mennonite background. Steeples, stained glass, and gorgeous architecture rise around and before me, suitcases and bags are familiar and are my armor. Yet, I am so ready for classes, so spiritually and emotionally hungry, so deeply wounded by life experiences and my own misconceptions of them, and so completely terrified.

Kyle chuckles knowingly, nodding his head for me to go on.

I briefly describe that first year and my mystification over all the talk of saints, pilgrims, contemplative spiritually, and centering prayer, clouds of unknowing, *lectio divina*, and mystics (*What on earth are Christian mystics?*).

I continue to describe how stunned I am by Christian history and themes I had never heard of, so much so I go through a phase of being angry. My church, parents, and culture hadn't taught me any of this. My friends and classmates talk about having spiritual directors; the conversations intrigue me and scare me half to death. I had learned early in life that my questions, angst, and searching were not appreciated, and I grew up swallowing and denying most of my longings and desires for God, and denying mystery and depth. The thought of purposely going to a religious authority so they can tell me what to believe and how to act is quite threatening! My friends speak lovingly about their spiritual processes and have such gratitude for their directors that curiosity overtakes me. Kairos offers free spiritual direction sessions for students. I sign up.

I tell Kyle how I picked a woman spiritual director who looks conservative: no jewelry, no frills in clothing or hair, and no makeup, and she wears a long braid down the middle of her back. She looks natural, like a Native American, walking softly upon the earth. She represents safety.

"She looks like your container!" Kyle laughs. We both laugh until I wipe tears from my eyes and he drops his head into his hands face down on the table in an effort to stop. Most of the house is in silence after dinner and even though talking is permitted in the basement area, sound echoes in this place of endless corridors and halls. We are conscious of making too much noise. Doesn't laughter expand when stifled! Similarly, curiosity mixed with holy desire expands us greatly in spite of our crazy fears. Kyle knows from personal experience and laughs in solidarity.

"Anyway," I begin again, "I creep into the room to meet this director woman. The room is way too small for my comfort. I need to stay far away from her. What if she is a crazy mystic and levitates or something? I'd freak." Kyle's shoulders start heaving with laughter, but he makes no sound. "I sit on a chair near the door, as far away from her as I can get. I even push the chair farther away when she looks down to adjust her sandals. As nervous as a first time flyer, I quickly find all possible escape routes and sit upright on the edge of my chair.

"She tells me about spiritual direction and lovingly answers my questions. She is comforting, nurturing, loving. She is patient and calm. She is love. Her eyes are small fires. Her beautiful soul shines through her skin. She is Christ to me. The room fades into the background, time evaporates; I'm devouring every word. I hear myself speaking, slowly but boldly. I am only aware of my openness, my desire to follow. Her path, her God, my path, my God; it all flows into one."

For a moment, I'm transported back to the beginnings of my more authentic journey, to this dear soul friend who loved me so much I was able to begin truly loving myself. I fall silent, now, savoring the memories. Kyle reverently holds the space with me.

"Our journeys are so sacred," I speak; he nods, sighs in contentment. For a long time we sit in silence.

Then suddenly, Kyle breaks the introspection: "You were actually afraid she'd levitate?" and we convulse with laughter again. He mumbles something about God laughing and falling off God's heavenly chair. We laugh until exhausted. Then, it's good night and God bless; we bow to each other, lovingly, prayerfully, and move off in separate directions, to our separate rooms and different lives, feeling touched by grace, connected, and deeply satisfied.

How cleansing it is to laugh, to let go of that yoke of taking ourselves and our religion so seriously, to envision a God who laughs with us. Not at us, not at our stupidity or ignorance, at our foibles or fears—just laughing in tune with our humanity. Our laughter honored our fears, the risks we take for personal and spiritual growth, the breaking of containers and the gathering of bigger containers around us for a while until we can bear more questions and mysteries and break out again into deeper unknowns. The beauty of coming together is always worth the chaos of falling apart; only Love gets us through the shattering and healing. Don't we all get goose bumps when experiencing Truth, or Beauty, or Genuine Presence? We can sit in solidarity with others more easily in the struggle, in the silence, and share depth and laughter too. Perhaps we can even find unity with all that lives and breathes to the extent that we are able to hold the mysteries of the universe without demanding that anything be solved.

CHAPTER 7

Connecting Heaven and Earth with Open Hearts

. . . . ## STRANDED ON AN ISLAND (DON)

I was nineteen years old and in my fourth month of a two-year Mennonite Voluntary Service (MVS) assignment in Honduras. It was my first month on my own trying to do my assigned job. I lived with another U.S. American MVSer on an isolated island about eighty miles off the north coast of Honduras. It was a beautiful Caribbean island settled by descendants of English pirates. The only transportation to the mainland was a daily overnight mail boat and an air service twice a day. My roommate and I felt rather remote from our headquarters in La Ceiba. There was no telephone service; the only way we could communicate with our fellow expatriate workers was by telegraph.

My job was to be an assistant to four credit unions and to see that their volunteer committees were functioning properly. I spent most of my time with the treasurers, making sure their books were properly kept and balanced. This was in the days before handheld calculators and computers. I had spent a month with the previous volunteer being oriented to the peculiarities of credit union bookkeeping. Right after he left, the largest of the four credit unions started experiencing a large cash deficit that kept increasing at the close of each day's business. We all assumed that it was an accounting problem, not that any of the volunteers could have been pilfering funds. However, as the expert from the United States, I was expected to find the problem and solve it.

I didn't have a clue what was wrong. I spent many days pouring over the receipts, the vouchers, and the entries into the accounting books without any luck. The problem kept growing along with my anxiety and their expectations of me. If the credit union cash deficit wasn't bad enough, my roommate, an agricultural extension agent, was away for a week visiting one of his projects.

In addition, several days before I had run into a U.S. tourist who reamed me out for being a conscientious objector (CO). He had lost his son in the Vietnam War. There I was, no one to talk to, no television to distract me, questioning my faith and reasons for doing what I was doing, wishing that I could either go home or die. I sat on the back stairs of our rented house and cried my heart out. I had never felt so alone in my life. I had a sense of Jesus' feeling of abandonment on the cross in his cry from Psalm 22:1-2:

> My God, my God, why have you forsaken me?
> Why are you so far from saving me,
> so far from my cries of anguish?
> My God, I cry out by day, but you do not answer,
> by night, but I find no rest.

ॐ

And the peace of God, which transcends
all understanding, will guard your hearts
and your minds in Christ Jesus. —Philippians 4:7

You will go out in joy
and be led forth in peace;
the mountains and hills
will burst into song before you,
and all the trees of the field
will clap their hands. —Isaiah 55:12

Existential Loneliness and Restlessness

The feeling that I experienced on that particular day on an isolated island in the middle of the Caribbean was loneliness. Although it was brought on by particular circumstances, our culture is rife with existential loneliness. This loneliness thwarts our psychological as well as spiritual growth and leaves us feeling abandoned and restless.

The evidence for this existential loneliness and restlessness is found in our obsessive-compulsive behaviors. We have a yearning for something more, and we try to fill the yearning with work, food—both overeating and under eating—drink, drugs, sex, entertainment, and even with healthy things like exercise and spiritual disciplines. I wrote at length about our culture of dissatisfaction and overconsumption in the chapters on abundance and gratitude; both are indicators of the void left by loneliness and restlessness.

I would like to describe five of what I consider to be the main causes: a loss of community, too much time on our hands, a loss of faith, separation from and exploitation of nature, and fragmentation.

Loss of Community

The loss of community began with the Industrial Revolution in the eighteenth century. People were attracted to cities where factories were springing up and providing employment. This trend continued through the nineteenth century and accelerated rapidly in the twentieth. As farming became more mechanized, the family farm, the most enduring economic unit for centuries, was almost completely replaced by the corporate farm. The unity of the rural community was broken.

In the United States, cities themselves retained a huge number of community enclaves as immigrants poured in to find work. These communities were often made up of a particular ethnic group, providing stability during difficult times of transition. Even though some of these communities survive to this day, the increasing desire to move to the suburbs in the latter part of the twentieth century has broken most remains of community in the cities.

With the industrial base of cities eroding, many young professionals are attracted to the city to find employment in the growing service industries: advertising, insurance, financial services, entertainment, online services, and so forth. Many young adults move away from their more rural communities after receiving a college degree. With this comes a separation from their families and other support systems, as well as the anonymity that comes with being a single face in a million. The potential to get lost in such a sea of humanity is high, and along with that they experience a loneliness that penetrates to the soul—an existential loneliness.

Before the urbanization and industrialization of the twentieth century, the church was the center of life in the village. Even in many of the ethnic enclaves in cities, the church was the center of life. Baptisms, confirmations, weddings, and funerals all brought the community together. Everyone generally knew everyone else. When something went wrong, everyone pitched in to help the family or person in need. With the break up of ethnic communities, the church as a community shaper and definer has mostly disappeared.

The rise of individual rights from the philosophies of the Enlightenment in the seventeenth and eighteenth centuries brought about loneliness as well. The individual is the center of all moral, philosophical, and even economic thought. While this emphasis on the individual has brought about many positive changes, it has made individualism next to a religion. We have been taught to rely on ourselves, that we are less of a person if we ask anyone for help. Because of this view, we tend to we hide our needs out of embarrassment until we reach a breaking point. Much of this could be avoided if we lived in true community.

Too Much Time on Our Hands

The move from small, labor-intensive farms to huge farms that are highly-mechanized, along with the Industrial Revolution, has resulted in having much more free time. City life brought shorter workweeks with free weekends. The Industrial Revolution brought labor-saving devices that freed up even more time. Having so much leisure time on our hands forced us to contemplate the meaning of our lives and our destiny. "Leisure time and affluence, because they have taken away from us the need to struggle to survive physically," writes Ronald Rolheiser, "have helped to throw us back upon ourselves and forced us to search for deeper meaning, interpersonal and spiritual."[1]

Used properly, the self-reflection stemming from all the free time on our hands could increase self-understanding and spirituality significantly. Too often, however, a void and a restlessness result, which we try to fill with the obsessions already mentioned: food, drink, drugs, sex, entertainment and the like, in addition to healthier fixations like working out and religious devotion. The advertising industry is adept at sending us messages to promise an end to our loneliness and has all sorts of solutions to fill our spare time. Unfortunately their solutions do not satisfy and only make the loneliness and restlessness more acute. Free time, instead of the blessing it could be, has become a curse and another cause of our existential loneliness.

Loss of Faith

With the church no longer at the center of community life, and with the rise of the discoveries of science and individualism during the Enlightenment, religious faith has been pushed farther into the background for a "modern" individual. The need for scientific verification and proof further eroded the sense of mystery and faith. Anything that couldn't be proved with the five senses wasn't real. Anything that couldn't be explained scientifically wasn't real. Reason triumphed over mysticism. Science had become the new religion.

"I think, therefore I am," declared the French philosopher Rene Descartes. Where once a person contemplated their being through a relationship with God and their "God-image-ness," now a person contemplates their existence through thinking. The brain had replaced the soul.

Separation from and Exploitation of Nature

The massive move from the farm to cities not only broke up communities, but also removed "modern" people from nature. Real vegetation was replaced by the "concrete jungle." This move to the city detached us from the source of our food supply and how dependent we are on nature for our very existence (food). The source of food is the supermarket, and animals are in zoos.

Industrialization had a voracious appetite for raw materials to produce goods for people with more money and more leisure time to spend it. The elimination of religion as a central principle to all of life took away guilt associated with our blatant exploitation of God's creation and goodness. On the other hand, religious conservatives sometimes claimed Scripture encourages dominion over creation. Nature was to be controlled and dominated by our minds, not to be tended by good stewards with a soul-connection to the created world. We view ourselves as above nature rather than as part of it. Although we pretend not to be aware of it, there is a longing within us to make peace with nature, to recognize our place within it. This longing is part of our existential loneliness.

Fragmentation

When we put all these causes of existential loneliness together, we arrive at a very fragmented person. We are separated from community, from faith, and from nature. We have time on our hands that we fill up with distractions, which only make us look for more exciting and entertaining ones. The brain has been separated from the soul. The resultant void tears at the deepest part of our being, but we push it aside. Restlessness develops that further fragments us.

Science and Greek thought separated the spiritual world from the material world. Socialization and modern life separated our work self from our home self. Other societal roles created personas (masks) that we use to define ourselves more than the way God created us to be. In order to function in our multifaceted world, we change our masks more often than we change our clothes. No wonder we feel pulled in so many directions. We are fragmented and long for wholeness and unity. This longing is existential loneliness.

Peace As a Remedy to Existential Loneliness and Restlessness

In my youth, before each communion service our church had what was called a "preparatory service" that was intended to prepare us to partake of the Eucharist. We were asked one question by our ordained leadership: "Are you at peace with God and your fellow man?" Everyone participating in the service had to respond individually to that question. Although for many it was another meaningless ritual, it sometimes brought out confessions and restored relationships. The practice was like a quarterly "consciousness examen." This practice has fallen by the wayside, which I think is a shame. We need to be more intentional today in our practice of partaking of the Lord's Supper.

Dealing with Our Restlessness and Longing for God

For dealing with our existential loneliness, I would like to add other parts to the pre-communion consciousness examen of my youth: Are you at peace with God, with yourself, with your fellow human beings, and with nature? Isaiah 55 of the Hebrew Scriptures provides us with some uncanny insights for helping us to deal with all of these questions.

"Come, all you who are thirsty," begins chapter 55. This identifies the restlessness and longing for God that is present in the human soul. Thirsting is a metaphor for a longing for God in other places in the Scripture as well, most notably in Psalm 42 with the deer panting for streams of water and John 4 with the woman at the well. When we consider that this holy longing was present even in ancient times, how much stronger it must be today with all the extra ingredients of existential loneliness that our "modern" societies have left us.

"Why spend money on what is not bread, and your labor on what does not satisfy?" implores Isaiah (Isaiah 55:2a). Trying to fill our restless, lonely God-void with unsatisfying purchases apparently is not just a modern phenomenon. It further identifies our need to be at peace with God and with ourselves.

Silence and Centering Prayer

Isaiah 55 continues: "Listen, listen to me, and eat what is good, and you will delight in the richest of fare. Give ear and come to me; listen, that you may live" (Isaiah 55:2b-3a). To be at peace with God and with ourselves, we need to stop our harried activity long enough to listen to God's still, small voice. What we will discover is a banquet prepared for us that will more than satisfy: a banquet that will quell our loneliness and help us to develop a more mellow spirit. Methods for stopping and listening to God are outlined in chapter 1 on overcoming cynicism with joy: active imagination, meditative walks, and music. I could also add centering prayer to this list. In centering prayer, one sits quietly for twenty minutes or longer and brings one's thoughts back to the "center" whenever they start to wander.

"Centering prayer is a method of silent prayer that prepares us to experience God's presence within us, closer than breathing, closer than thinking, closer than consciousness itself," states the website centeringprayer.com. This intimacy helps us understand how much God loves us, making peace with God and with ourselves more possible. Basking in God's love through silence makes us at peace with ourselves as well.

Covenant with God
"I will make an everlasting covenant with you, my faithful love promised to David. See, I have made him a witness to the peoples, a ruler and commander of the peoples" (Isaiah 55:3b-4). God now moves from the personal to the communal. Are you at peace with your fellow human beings? Jesus' covenanted community gathers around his table to share the cup and the bread. As important as it is to sit in silence as individuals to establish a relationship with God, it is just as important to gather together with other people. This community helps us to mitigate the extreme individualism of our culture and is the basis for mutual aid—both physical and spiritual. It's where beggars gather to tell each other where to find bread.

Covenant with Others
But our gathering is to prepare us for scattering and sharing. "Surely you will summon nations you know not, and nations you do not know will come running to you, because of the Lord your God, the Holy One of Israel, for he has endowed you with splendor" (Isaiah 55:5). The banquet feast is for everyone, not just for the children of Israel or for the members of Jesus' community. The abundance is for all. Therefore, it needs to be shared.

Sharing God's abundance has always been a problem for trying to be at peace with our fellow human beings. Too often humans gather to draw lines to define who gets and who does not get God's abundance. What is freely given to be freely shared is often hoarded.

These lines and hoarding inevitably cause conflict. Isaiah reminds us to "seek the Lord while he may be found; call on him while he is near. Let the wicked forsake their ways and the unrighteous their thoughts. Let them turn to the Lord, and he will have mercy on them, and to our God, for he will freely pardon" (Isaiah 55:6-7). The wicked and the unrighteous in my view are the hoarders—those who want to exclude others from the banquet feast. To have peace with our fellow human beings they must "turn to the Lord, and he will have mercy on them." Indeed, not only do they need to turn to the Lord, but we also all need to turn to each other to forgive each other. We will write more about mercy and forgiveness in a later chapter.

Covenant with Nature

Finally, are you at peace with nature? Again we turn to Isaiah 55: "As the rain and the snow come down from heaven, and do not return to it without watering the earth and making it bud and flourish, so that it yields seed for the sower and bread for the eater, so is my word that goes out from my mouth: It will not return to me empty, but will accomplish what I desire and achieve the purpose for which I sent it" (vv. 10-11). The relationship between God and creation is intimate. In order to know God we need to know creation. John Philip Newell in his book *Christ of the Celts* writes about nature's importance. "The great Irish teacher John Scotus Eriugena taught that God speaks to us in two books. One is the little book, he says, the book of scripture, physically little. The other is the big book, the book of creation, as vast as the universe."[2]

I could write volumes about how Western civilization has pillaged and abused nature, mostly for material gain. We have much to learn from indigenous peoples from around the globe on how to make peace with nature. They start by having respect and reverence for nature, not worshiping it, in spite of what many "modern" Christians would purport. "[They] celebrate the presence of God in the elements," writes Newell, "but do not confuse God with creation."[3] This celebration promotes reverence and awe for creation rather than exploitation and destruction. The story is often told of Native Americans asking a deer for forgiveness before killing it for food. This clearly shows the reverence they have for nature and their place in it. As part of nature we are codependent.

In order to quell our restlessness, to deal with our existential loneliness, we need to make peace with God, with ourselves, with our fellow human beings, and with nature. This peace, which according to Philippians 4:7 "transcends all understanding, will guard your hearts and minds in Christ Jesus." Guarding your heart means making it more open and receptive. Isaiah describes this spaciousness like this: "You will go out in joy and be led forth in peace; the mountains and hills will burst into song before you, and all the trees of the field will clap their hands" (Isaiah 55:12). Our lives are more whole and nature celebrates. Our heartbeats are joined as one. This is Jesus' kingdom come "on earth as it is in heaven" (Matthew 6:10). It has come and will last forever. The final words of Isaiah 55 bear this out: "This will be for the Lord's renown, for an everlasting sign, that will endure forever" (v. 13b).

ॐ

EXPERIENCING GOD: MAKING PEACE WITH LIFE AS IT UNFOLDS (SHARON)

One morning while brushing my teeth, I reached up to scratch a spot off the bathroom mirror and instantly noticed some extra fullness under my arm. I froze for a second, then dropped the toothbrush and tentatively felt around for a lump. Three years into remission from lymphoma, this was no small matter.

Now, a week later, I'm lying on an ultrasound table, left arm raised up over my head, the technician resting his arm on my belly to steady his hand as he reaches across my body to take images. Suddenly, I can't breathe under the weight of his arm. His touch, our human connection coupled with my vulnerability and his kind words, makes this all too real. I want to scream. I want to disappear. I want to get away from this pressure! I'm aware my breath has turned shallow from the chest instead of deep from my belly, and is triggering a bodily reaction of "run, run away!"

Noticing my very human reaction of fight or flight, I instantly fall into practicing the prayer of welcome: *Welcome, fear, welcome. This fear belongs.* In saying yes to life I embrace knowing life includes things that are out of my control. *I let go of my need for health, happiness, and security. I let go of my need to change this situation.* I allow fear to settle in, feeling it, but not identifying with it. My thoughts race; I just let them be. After a few minutes my body relaxes, my breathing eases. I'm grateful when the technician lifts his arm up, and I wait calmly as he adjusts the machine. Then he leaves to speak to the radiologist. I lay there breathing easily when a thought—*This is so not fair!*—completely captures me and every muscle tenses. My shoulders pull up tight; my fingers curl. I choose to soften my hands, open them, and go back through the welcoming cycle: *Welcome, anger, welcome. This anger belongs. I let go of my need to have things go the way I think they should go.* I change my thoughts: *All is well. I am safe. This bed I'm laying on supports me, the sheets smell wonderful, my body is delightfully made and is programed for healing.*

I wrote the above story months ago. I still marvel at the divine grace that empowered my welcoming. I fail at this so often during the ups and downs of my regular living. Though this kind of welcoming is difficult during fearful situations and takes much practice on many smaller challenges first, this is the stance I desire to take in life: open palm, open heart. Yes, this too is part of my journey, my becoming more present and spacious. Beyond my likes and dislikes, life is about returning. Returning to my center, the deepest, truest part of myself, the place where I abide in Love. This space, in all of us, has the capacity to grow so deep and wide that heaven and earth connect. It is the place of love and stillness, where nothing can disturb the whole or upset the balance. Winds of emotion and opinion may blow and storm on the surface, but deep in my center there is only presence, awareness, belonging, safety, and an exquisite nothing, which contains everything.

Returning to my center is not repressing or avoiding thoughts or emotions. On the ultrasound table, I acknowledged fear and anger. By doing so, I was able to move into, and through, to *beyond* my thoughts and emotions to a deeper place of abiding. This process is taking the practice of centering prayer and living it by noticing and, without judgment, embracing what arises in me, then letting go enough to choose my response rather than simply reacting. Centering in love, in my understanding of God, I can always be okay inside no matter what is happening on the outside.

When I dwell on the surface, on the various details of my life, I prefer health, happiness, security, and harmony; when I come home to my center, there is truly no preference. I am grateful for each day, with or without cancer. The lump that brought me to the ultrasound table turned out to be a swollen tendon, not lymphoma. The diagnosis became inconsequential after all the welcoming, owning of my fears, and going through them to my peaceful center. This practice made it easier to really listen to my body. I felt sure cancer was not returning, so I had already moved on. This welcoming practice reminds me I'm always in the process of dying, both physically and in letting go of my demands for happiness. When I'm identified with love at my center, I'm not identified with the particulars of my life.

A dear friend told her husband about the "prayer of welcoming" after I described it to her. Intrigued, she tried it out for a month. The next time we met, she described how seemingly impossible yet attractive this prayer is to her and her spouse. Her husband calls it the "here we go again" prayer. We laughed in agreement, knowing life gives us constant opportunities to practice getting over ourselves, identifying ourselves with all our thoughts, feelings, opinions, and likes/dislikes. We find our truest selves in that wide, open, still, spacious place centered in love, goodness, beauty, and truth. As author Paula D'Arcy likes to say, God usually comes to us disguised as our life.

The prayer of welcoming, explained so eloquently by Cynthia Bourgeault in her book, *Centering Prayer and Inner Awakening*, and other contemplative practices help us reflect in healthy ways. These practices help us make peace with ourselves, with others, nature, and with God by giving greater clarity for what might need changing, what might need some loving attention, what our truest response to life's difficulties may be, what action to take, what needs letting go, and when we need to immerse ourselves in gratitude for earth's beauty. This is one way to return home to ultimate love and safety—home to the heart of God where we experience peace rather than understand it.

Experiencing God: Stories of Longing, Seeking, Experiencing

A young man sits by the window staring at empty city streets. He brushes away strands of hair past sleepy eyes, glances at the babe tucked into the sofa—one tiny arm wrestled free of her blanket and thrown carelessly above the tousled curls on her head. She is so delicately perfect and so asleep after the outrage of midnight colic. His hungry eyes drink in the calm outside, the silent streets, and the moon glow on windows above the planter boxes that pour tiny blue lobelia flowers down brick walls. The house feels calm too, despite dirty dishes piled in the sink, textbooks spread haphazardly across the small table pulled up against the sofa to protect the sprawling infant from falling, and a coffee mug etching damp rings into wood. He sighs; if only his soul were calm. His soul feels shattered like broken glass, the shards strewn about, and he is lost and aching to come together. He longs for a place to be real, to be safe, a place where he can express his doubts and questions. He wonders if others struggle as he does, if anyone else wants more from life: not more achieving, or more stuff, but more meaning and honesty. He thinks of the little church around the corner and briefly imagines what kind of people might be there.

Miles away from the city and hours before the young father will sit staring out the window, past suburbia, across meadows and wheat fields, down a small country road, and inside a tiny, ornate chapel, a sixty-year-old woman squirms to the edge of the lemon-oiled wooden pew and kneels, bringing her hands to the prayer position. She stares at the beautiful stained glass above the sanctuary cross; the weight of her prayer fills the empty space. She remembers the beauty of vespers music, the aroma of candle wax burning, and the loving faces of her community. *Why is it not enough?* she wonders. *I'm so grateful for my family, my church; blessed with so much, yet I long for more.* She waits, soul trembling, hoping for insight.

It comes in the form of deep soul-aching loneliness. A sob catches in her throat as she recognizes and names this awareness. It would be overwhelming if not for a simultaneous sense of love, a drawing into deep love that comforts her. She trusts this drawing and raises her head and heart to listen. In time, she begins to understand the loneliness. She tells God her desire for depth, authenticity, and purpose. She longs to be known, really known and accepted for where she is on her life journey. She does not want to be taught, advised, or told what to do and believe, but simply wants companionship. She longs to share deeply, more authentically, with others and be safe. She knows she is made for this. She intuitively knows all humanity is made for this. But where does one go to find such safety, such mutual relating that isn't just about church rules, theology and correct thinking, politeness, or denominational-approved praying or speaking?

Deep in prayer, the woman startles when the custodian enters the chapel, rattling his ring of keys. She gets up to leave, knowing her longing for deeper community will be her prayer for some time.

Two teenagers climb the small town water tower at midnight, daring each other on, laughing, joking, all at a whisper so the neighborhood dogs keep their howls in their throats instead of out through their equally bored mouths. Shelly suddenly freezes; Nick looks in the direction she's pointing. Their bodies respond with silence and awe as their eyes track the blaze of a shooting star. In the next instant, they are filled with the astounding beauty of the night sky. Like a hug, they feel the brilliance of stars and caress of moon. Boundaries lose their edges. Time, objects, and space soften and blur for a second. The teens aren't sure if they are human or stardust or sky or sleeping dogs, yet they are very awake and alive. The two become simultaneously many, or one, or at the very least, two experiencing one completely whole moment.

Then as unexpectedly as it came, the moment ends. Both catch their breath, feeling the loss sharply. Their eyes meet; they know whatever this was they experienced it together. They know it is indescribable except for what it is not: not romance, not joy, not a high, not anything they can name, not even anything remarkable. Or is it? They look around self-consciously; suddenly they are aware of their separateness and how pointless and unnatural it seems. After an awkward pause they silently, sheepishly, begin moving down the ladder.

All of these stories are about real people, real longings for depth, intimacy, and community. Their names, situations, and experiences are changed, compiled, or rearranged for privacy, and then the details are tossed up like confetti but forever caught in my heart and soul. I understand the soul hunger—the desire to be deeply known and accepted. I cherish these stories and allow them to open me.

Stories change the way I see humanity, the universe, and spirituality. I marvel at how the Spirit of God entices, draws, and moves people's hearts. The power of love and awakening always touches me as I listen to people's stories. I listen with spiritual senses as well as physical senses, with the desire to hear where God is active in someone's life. Our stories unite us more than divide us; we would all feel much less alone if we could truly listen to one another with open hearts and minds. Listen and accept without the need to fix, rescue, save, change the storyteller, or impress the teller with our theology or experiences. Listen with our trust firmly centered in God's ability to draw people, to change lives, and not in our own ability to influence the teller's life or faith. The sheer ability to listen to each other's stories, without so much of our own commentary, is transformative to both teller and listener.

Openness and deep listening to each other unites us in the human family, the church family, with God and Mystery. Listening helps us let go of overidentification with our own dramas and inner commentaries and helps us hold the tension of all that is unresolved. Let's not wait for others to make it safe for us to be real, to share and listen deeply; let's just become a safe haven for ourselves and offer the same to others. While it is validating to be heard with acceptance and compassion, sometimes we forget we can be that for ourselves first. When we are more compassionate and authentic with ourselves, it becomes easier to share deeply with others and with God. There is a time and a place for teaching or evangelism, of course, but the church is often experienced there and inexperienced with raw authenticity and deeper listening. This is the church's growing edge.

The stories I've shared are unpolished and unfinished. Does the young man go to the church down the road? If he does, will he be welcomed and his soul integrated, or will he be seen mostly as a fish for a zealous religious hook? Will the woman find deepening intimacy with others on the spiritual journey? Will she find this inside or outside her church? Do the two teenagers remember their experience with mystery and oneness? Are they drawn toward the beauty of the night sky like wondrous toddlers seeing stars for the first time? Will anyone tell them they had an experience of God or if they dare share their stories will others dismiss their encounter because they never experienced God in such a way, so it can't be Divine?

As we listen reverently to each other's stories and honor our own, we get better at holding the pull of our struggles: what is unfinished, the chaos of creativity, the unperfected. We become less demanding; we trust the process of transformation, the way Divine Love heals, and all of this adds to the continual journey of becoming spiritually awakened. We become more open, aware, more creative, accepting, and spiritually mature.

The still, small voice of God is not always still and not always small, just as earth's splendor is not always subdued. In my practice, I often see a God who speaks loudly and humorously, yet most of us are too busy to bother, too restless to notice, or don't have well-developed spiritual eyes and ears. It is us who need to be still and learn to cultivate the ability to listen and see. Often, God speaks so intimately, so lovingly, and so in line with our own beauty and potential that we dismiss and overlook the encounter because we don't really know ourselves that well. Or we expect God to show up differently. And, we are simply afraid to look. We fear God encounters. We fear getting to know ourselves, others, and the earth intimately. Our fears are understandable because if we get to know ourselves deeply, we might want to grow, or heal the earth, and we might actually love ourselves. Often we've been taught to avoid self-love for fear of pride or selfishness. Women especially have internalized the message of selflessness to the point of becoming too sacrificial, developing unhealthy boundaries or a victim/martyr complex.

Even as churches and schools develop programs for spiritual formation, most of my clients are hungry for instruction in prayer forms, self-awareness, reflection, authenticity and integrity, personal discernment, body awareness, and earth appreciation. Spiritual practices like centering prayer, the prayer of welcoming, *lectio divina*, and other contemplative prayers, along with deep listening to each other, help us trust our own processes and the action of God in our lives. These practices help lessen our fears of selfishness, pride, and narcissism. As we reflect and become self-aware we can see ourselves more clearly, both our beauty and our self-delusions. We can see how we are divinely made, how we can be Christ to each other. Like the story of the velveteen rabbit sharing love, sharing our stories is what makes us real.

The next story illustrates how amazingly close God is to us at all times, and how Hannah found her way home to ultimate safety into the heart of God. Hannah is a retreatant for a directed silent retreat I'm leading at Kairos: School of

Spiritual Formation. She sits across from me, smiling. She is the picture of peace and contentment: face aglow, body relaxed, shoulders down, breath coming from deep in her core. We sit together in silence, savoring her story, her "God smiles" as I like to call such experiences of divine consolation.

Earlier in the weekend, she told me of her struggle to connect with God. She is no stranger to silence and solitude, but a while back her life took a crazy turn and not only does she struggle to flow with it, she struggles to find time for quiet reflection. Rather than feeling God's presence in her midst, she feels overwhelmed, abandoned, and scared. It's admirable, I told her, that she is giving herself this gift of rest and solitude. After listening awhile, I heard a longing to lighten up and not take life so seriously tucked within the folds of her story, so I invited her to spend some time over the weekend remembering when she was young, what she liked to do. Then, perhaps she could play a little and invite God to play with her. She laughed, wondering how one plays with God.

When we met later, she brought me a simple line drawing, in color pencil, of two trapeze artists. One was gracefully free-flying through the air, arms outstretched. The other swung on the opposite side of her paper, arms also outstretched, but this figure had very large hands, with fingers spread wide, anticipating the catch. The picture was so simple, so honest and graceful that my own heart soared and caught while gazing prayerfully at it. Hannah said she was a gymnast when she was young. Her drawn lines were curved and flowing, yet the picture captured perfectly those breathless, wild moments after letting go and flying through the air before being securely caught and held.

Hannah labeled the catcher with the big hands God. She was the flier. Like every relationship, there is both holding on and letting go. Hannah talked about needing to discard her overly serious adult self and just play, if only for a moment or two. Mostly though, her drawing represented how God shows up when she is able to open her spiritual eyes. God is always ready to connect. Always loving her, waiting for the invitation to love, to play with her, to partner with her in life's doings and catch and hold her heart. The catch represented home, her spiritual center, where all is well on the inside no matter what is happening on the outside. The letting go represented playfulness and trust. Her drawing, her experience, is such a beautiful example of how all of us can encounter God anywhere, in any way, and intimately so if the eyes of our hearts are open: how we can come home and truly experience divine peace rather than cognitively understand it.

CHAPTER 8

Where Is Your Heart?

LOST VISA (DON)

I was leading a group of students through Mexico for a month of study. We ended our month in Mexico City, and on the last day of our trip I discovered that one of our students had lost her visa. It is impossible to leave Mexico without this visa, so if we wanted to return to the United States, we had one day to do something about it. I thought that I could use my language skills and cultural know-how to remedy the situation in a few hours. I jumped into a taxi and took off to the office that I was told would come to our aid. I visited one office after another. Every office I visited gave me a different story and sent me on to another office.

Our day was quickly coming to an end, and I was still no closer to a solution than when I began. The situation was out of my hands. I was not in control. Our fate was in the hands of some unknown authority in some yet unknown office somewhere in the largest city in the world. What should I do? Send the other students home on our regularly scheduled flight and stay with the student in Mexico City until the situation got resolved? Return home with the other students and make the guilty student stay behind to resolve the situation herself? Who would pick up the extra expenses to be incurred? My budget was basically shot since we were at the end of the trip. There were no easy solutions to my dilemma; I was at my wit's end.

As a last resort, I took my student to the one place that I figured offered the most hope for our dire situation. Instead of accompanying her with my superior language and cultural know-how, I told her to go to such-and-such an office and cry her heart out while explaining her situation—cry like she had never cried before. Within a half hour she returned with the necessary papers to return to the United States the next day with the rest of our group.

Developing a spacious heart means letting go of our need to be in control.

≥≉

Who, being in very nature God,
did not consider equality with God something to be used
to his own advantage;
rather, he made himself nothing
by taking the very nature of a servant,
being made in human likeness.
And being found in appearance as a man,
he humbled himself
by becoming obedient to death—
even death on a cross! —Philippians 2:6-8

My Father, if it is possible, may this cup be taken from me. Yet not as I will, but as you will. —MATTHEW 26:39B

Whoever finds his life will lose it, and whoever loses his life for my sake will find it. —MATTHEW 10:39

Control Freaks

We live in a culture of control freaks, and I am exhibit A of this tendency. I have my daily routine that I hate to have disrupted for anything. This allows me to be in control. I tolerate holidays, birthdays, and anniversaries but do not like how they interrupt my routine. I don't like surprises. The twelve-inch snowstorm that rolled through the Shenandoah Valley where I live when I wrote this really upset my schedule. I lost control of my day.

When you travel to other countries, you have the least control over your personal life. Language, social mores, host families, and friends all have different expectations on how to negotiate a daily schedule. You become dependent on others to navigate the day. I have learned how to let go of my routines after many years of living in both Latin America and Europe, but the lessons have not come easily.

I married a woman from Switzerland and we spent the first year of our marriage in her country. At the beginning, I knew very little of the language and customs and was totally dependent on her to do the simplest of tasks: arrange for our marriage with all the legal papers, find a place to rent, set up our utilities, and look for a job for me. I felt helpless. I felt unmanly. I had no control and was totally dependent. This is not how I wanted to be or to feel. This is not how I was socialized to exist.

At the beginning of the chapter I recounted the story of a student losing her visa. There is no question that I had no control of the situation I faced. The longer the day went by without resolution, the more frustrated I became. I was at the mercy of a system that in spite of what I thought, I knew little about. I'm sure that this frustration was evident to the officials in the various offices I visited, and they probably made the process more difficult because they enjoyed seeing a U.S. American at their mercy. I'm sure that my blood pressure was sky-high. My mental and emotional states were anything but mellow.

Both of these incidents highlight how being in another culture can knock the control freak props out from under us. In spite of how uncomfortable both of these situations made me, they also taught me the most about my need for control and how to deal with it in a healthier way.

Self-Emptying and Service

Contrast my state of being, especially in the story from Mexico City, with that of the man I wrote about in "Where Is Your Heart?"[1] an article for *The Mennonite*, the official paper of Mennonite Church USA. Antonio lives in a middle-to-lower-middle class neighborhood in the northern part of Mexico City. His neighborhood is riddled with crime, gangs, drugs, alcoholism, unemployment, and underemployment. Antonio is a trained dentist, but he only works half days in his practice.

Antonio divides his normal days (although it could be argued that there are no normal days in his life) between his family business and his dental practice. His family business consists of making specialty soaps in the garage of his house. He spends time during the morning overseeing this business and providing jobs for a number of unemployable neighbors and family members. In the afternoons, he sees patients at his dental practice, which is housed several blocks away in the home of his mother.

You'd think that a dentist would earn enough money that no supplemental income would be needed. But Antonio is not your typical dentist. He sees many patients who cannot afford dental work. He does their care for a minimal fee, or for free. His dentist's office is lined with before-and-after pictures of numerous children with extreme orthodontic issues, fixed by his handiwork. Many of these children were picked on in school and on the street because of their teeth. Few could afford the price of normal dental services, let alone the normally exorbitant costs of these special needs. Antonio's skill and compassion for the poor changed all that.

In spite of all this activity, Antonio always has time for his neighbors. I've accompanied him several times on foot through his neighborhood. We would walk between his house, the church, and his dental practice. He has an uncanny sense of what is going on in the lives of his neighbors. When he knows something is not normal, he stops and talks. He asks them to come to church, to meet him for breakfast or coffee, and on many occasions, he stops in the middle of the street and prays for the person in need. Interruptions for him are not irksome: they are opportunities for ministry. Antonio models servanthood like few other people I have known.

People who don't understand Antonio's motivations as a child of God consider him to be crazy. He could move to a better neighborhood, or move his dental practice to a better neighborhood and make enough money to be set for life. But Antonio holds his life lightly. He gives away his life in service to others. Most people in the U.S. American culture, like me, want to hold on tightly to our lives, to be in control. We say we believe in God and his providence, but in the final analysis, we believe more in our abilities to provide for ourselves.

Gelassenheit and Self-Emptying

The Anabaptists, from the radical wing of the sixteenth century Reformation and forebears of the Mennonite Church, had a wonderful German word for holding one's life lightly: *Gelassenheit.* This word is so rich in meaning that there is not a direct word for it in English. According to the *Global Anabaptist Encyclopedia Online*, these are the multiple meanings of the word: "self-surrender, resignation in God's will, yieldedness to God's will, self-abandonment, the (passive) opening to God's willing, including the readiness to suffer for the sake of God, also peace and calmness of mind."[2]

In my view, Antonio embodies *Gelassenheit*. *Gelassenheit* is the embodiment of a spacious heart.

The last part of the definition of *Gelassenheit* is especially intriguing for our discussion. The phrases "the readiness to suffer for the sake of God, also peace and calmness of mind," seem to be a contradiction in terms. How can a readiness to suffer be placed together with peace and calmness of mind? Many spiritual truths are indeed paradoxical. A perfect example of this comes from Matthew 10:39: "Whoever finds his life will lose it, and whoever loses his life for my sake will find it." From verses like these, the Anabaptists developed their concept of *Gelassenheit*, and their ultimate role model was Jesus himself.

Jesus and *Gelassenheit*

Jesus embodied *Gelassenheit*, or "peace and calmness of mind," better than any other human being in history. He was ready to "suffer for the sake of God" as well. Indeed he ultimately died fulfilling God's will. It didn't come without struggle, however. In his prayer in the garden of Gethsemane, he cried out to God in Matthew 26:39: "My Father, if it is possible, may this cup be taken from me." His totally human side was begging to be freed from what lay ahead. But because of his *Gelassenheit*, he was able to let his life go, to quit holding on to it so tightly, and to yield his will to that of the sovereign God. He followed his human plea with the prayer, "Yet not as I will, but as you will" (Matthew 26:39). He totally surrendered his human will to the will of God. This is self-abandonment; this is *Gelassenheit*.

Exhibiting his *Gelassenheit*, Jesus also gave up his celestial home and "made his dwelling among us" (John 1:14). A hymn to this *Gelassenheit* is recorded in Philippians 2:6-8:

> Who, being in very nature God, did not consider equality with God something to be used to his own advantage; rather, he made himself nothing by taking the very nature of a servant, being made in human likeness. And being

found in appearance as a man, he humbled himself by
becoming obedient to death—even death on a cross!

It is hard for us to wrap our finite minds around this
event, this embodiment, this incarnation, this perfect example of how to live with an open heart.

Jesus and Self-Emptying

Even if you believe that Jesus was simply a good religious
teacher and was not the Son of God, there is something utterly unique about his ministry. Cynthia Bourgeault writes
about this in her book *The Wisdom Jesus.* "In whatever life
circumstance, Jesus always responded with the same motion
of self-emptying," she writes, "or to put it another way, of
the same motions of descent: going lower, taking the lower
place, not the higher."[3] This self-emptying is *Gelassenheit.*
This self-emptying, always taking the lower place, is unique
among religious teachers. Again, from Bourgeault: "For the
vast majority of the world's spiritual seekers, the way to God
is 'up.' Deeply embedded in our religious and spiritual traditions—and most likely in the human collective unconscious
itself—is a kind of compass that tells us that the spiritual
journey is an ascent, not a descent."[4]

This self-emptying and servant posture of Jesus not only
embodies *Gelassenheit,* but it also confirms for me the claim
that Jesus is the "way, the truth and the life" (John 14:6). I
believe that God has revealed truth in all world religions, but
this element of descent rather than ascent makes Jesus the
ultimate revelation of God.

Jesus took this posture of yieldedness, of self-renuncia-
tion, of *Gelassenheit,* of being completely in the will of God,
all the way to the cross. Being totally dependent on God, being perfectly in his will, even to suffering and death, gave him
perfect peace: a perfectly open heart.

As such, Jesus demonstrated to us the most integrated,
the most fulfilled, the most complete, and the least fragmented human being who ever lived. If we believe that Jesus was

totally human, and I do, it is astounding to consider that he became such a totally self-surrendered individual. If we believe that he was totally human, then we have within us the same potential to become as self-surrendered as he: to lose our life in order to gain it. We like to deny this possibility by saying that Jesus was also fully divine, making him more capable than we. However, this negates what we say we believe about him.

Withdrawing to Pray

So how do we develop *Gelassenheit*? How can we learn to lose our life in order to gain it? We have some models around us like Antonio the dentist, but the best way is to look to Jesus himself. He followed many of the spiritual disciplines that we have been writing about in this book. First, Jesus began his ministry by spending forty days in the desert, fasting and praying. The scriptural record doesn't tell us exactly what he did during those forty days, but we can use our imaginations. I think he spent many hours in silence, used active imagination, and went on meditative walks like I described in chapter 1. However he spent his time, it is clear that he came out of the experience with a clear sense of his call and his mission.

In Luke 6:12, it is recorded that "Jesus went out to a mountainside to pray, and spent the night praying to God." Like the desert and mountainside experiences, to follow Jesus' example, the first thing that we need to do is to spend time in retreat and develop our relationship with God. Perhaps we don't need to spend a complete forty days, nor do we need to go to the desert, but we need to take time for retreat, fasting, and prayer, with an emphasis on retreat. Whether a weekend, a week, or a month, a retreat from the distractions of everyday life is of utmost importance in developing *Gelassenheit* and a spacious heart. Although retreats that focus on issues of spirituality are good and necessary, I am talking about retreats without any agenda: retreats that offer times in solitude for reflection, for prayer, and for discernment. Only as we do this will it be possible to hear a clear call from God and to surrender ourselves completely to God's direction.

Jesus continued his intimate relationship with God through numerous times of withdrawing to pray, even during the busiest days of his ministry. "Very early in the morning, while it was still dark, Jesus got up, left the house and went off to a solitary place, where he prayed," says Mark 1:35. Withdrawal, retreat, and prayer help you maintain an intimate relationship with God, surrender to God's will, and learn to embody *Gelassenheit*.

Community

Jesus also established a community of believers. Continuing the story in Luke 6:13: "When morning came, he called his disciples to him and chose twelve of them, whom he also designated apostles." These twelve disciples he gathered around himself to teach, for support, and to work alongside him in his ministry. This was Jesus' community of faith: his small group, cell, or support group.

Jesus' ministry worked not only at healing the sick and casting out demons, but also at confronting the social justice issues of his day. He frequently had run-ins with the religious authorities who were more concerned about keeping their laws than caring for the fatherless and the widows. Nothing illustrates this better than Jesus' cleansing of the temple (Matthew 21:12-13; Mark 11:15-17; John 2:12-22).

Jesus' community was also involved in outreach: the spreading of the good news. In Matthew 10 he commissioned his community to go out on their own to do ministry in his name, and he warned them of the trouble they would run into with the authorities because of their work. In spite of the importance of a personal devotional life and intimacy with God, one cannot function alone. The support of a community of faith becomes very important in developing the self-emptying posture needed for *Gelassenheit*.

Nature

Jesus was also attuned to nature like no other. Calming the storm (Mark 4:35-41), walking on water (Matthew 14:22-33), and helping the disciples catch an abundance of fish (John 21:1-14) are just a few examples of his relationship with nature. In addition, most of his stories, parables, and illustrations came from nature. To become the most integrated person to walk the face of the earth, Jesus had to know his place in nature. He was not alienated from nature as most of us modern people are, as discussed in the chapter on existential loneliness. He was at peace with nature as he was at peace with God.

A Spacious Heart

Finally, Jesus exhibited an open heart. He didn't allow himself to be burdened with the excesses of the law of the Jews, seemingly breaking them without much thought about the consequences (see Luke 6:1-10). In Luke 7:34, he was accused of being a partier. "The Son of Man came eating and drinking, and you say, 'Here is a glutton and a drunkard, a friend of tax collectors and sinners.'" It seems that he had the perfect balance between taking seriously his mission as God's son, and holding his life lightly. "For my yoke is easy and my burden is light," he says in Matthew 11:30.

This is in direct contrast to the burden laid upon the followers of the Pharisaic law. In popular parlance, Jesus is "laid back." He identifies his mellow heart in the preceding verse: "for I am gentle and humble in heart." A gentle heart is another way to describe a mellow heart. This mellowness and gentleness of heart leads to a healthy spirituality: one that will give you "rest for your souls" (Matthew 11:30b).

It is difficult to "lose one's life in order to gain it." It is difficult to relinquish our need to be in control. It is difficult to espouse all the traits of *Gelassenheit* to which the Anabaptists aspired. It takes effort to follow the perfect example of Jesus, the one who modeled these kingdom qualities better than anyone else.

Because of how difficult it is to "let go," we can get down on ourselves for our human failings. Getting down on ourselves, however, is not being mellow of heart. Instead, we take ourselves too seriously and hold on too tightly to our lives. Our attitude should be more like Paul's in Philippians 3:12: "Not that I have already obtained all this [*Gelassenheit*], or have already arrived at my goal [total surrender], but I press on to take hold of that for which Christ Jesus took hold of me."

ॐ

.... **EXPERIENCING GOD: AN ANGEL IN A FUR COAT (SHARON)**
As a shy child in a large family, I always took a seat firmly positioned on the sidelines of our activities. Since my own opinions formed only after much introspection—after a day or even weeks after an argument or an event—few were patient enough to ask me what I thought. I grew up believing I didn't have an opinion. Often I became confused and befuddled over the arguments, the jockeying for position, the determination to succeed, win, or persuade the other. I simply didn't care that much. By the time I was born, sibling pecking order was well entrenched, so I also grew up believing I had little control over anything. I reached maturity fairly certain I was not a control freak. The following story illustrates the opposite.

A month ago, while skimming through Facebook, I came across the photo of a golden haired beauty of a dog, a large German Shepherd mix. My heart did an odd leap at the sight of her. The photo was posted to the Virginia Dog Rescue (VDR), and came through to my own Facebook wall, even though their page had not been working properly for weeks. Months before, Jay and I decided to stop fostering dogs awaiting adoption through this program. I had given away all my extra dog supplies, so this reaction intrigued me. Was this just a ping of sadness over the end of an era?

Curious, I brought up VDR's page on my computer and scrolled down through the photos and updates. The golden haired dog photo appeared with comments; I clicked on the photo to read the comments, but got only a message that the comments were no longer available. The only information I gleaned was her name, Cobie. I left it at that.

Days passed. The dog popped into my awareness over and over, unbidden, in the middle of washing dishes, playing hide and seek with grandson Jude, even amid times of concentration on creative projects. I emailed Connie, the rescue coordinator, and asked for more information about Cobie.

Connie gave me the stats: Cobie was a Shepherd mix weighing around eighty-five pounds. The owners were threatening to put her in the local shelter, and there were no foster homes available. I wanted to foster this dog, and I dreaded explaining myself to Jay. We discussed her size, the total inappropriateness of bringing a strange dog into our house while our small grandson's face was still healing from the scars of a dog attack three months before. Jay said no, and I respected his answer, telling Connie we'd decided against fostering Cobie. I asked to be kept informed. Since fostering was not an option, I just held this dog gently in my heart, in my prayers. I felt strongly nudged to put her photo as wallpaper on my computer. Naturally I talked to her whenever I saw the photo. *You are loved. Don't be afraid. All will be well.*

Two weeks later, Connie informed me there was still no foster home for Cobie; the rescue program would have to put her in boarding as she could no longer remain where she was. I was concerned as money going into long-term boarding takes resources away from dogs needing rescue. I talked to Jay again, telling him something was urging me to take this dog. Bless his heart; he trusts my intuition. So we agreed to foster her if four conditions were met. That Cobie must be gentle with children, transported directly to me, a crate must be provided, and that Connie must agree to keep looking for a long-term foster home. I made it clear I was only considering myself a short-term emergency foster.

Jubilantly, Connie set the system in motion and three days later, Cobie arrived on our farm, transported from southern

Virginia to Pennsylvania. The last driver in a succession of drivers coaxed a bewildered-looking big dog out of his vehicle and handed me her leash and a bag containing a small amount of kibble, some medications, and her vet records. I took the leash and instead of the expected joyful meeting, I felt an onslaught of fearful confusion. The dog I talked to in the photo was a sunlit blonde puppy; this girl was mature, with the dark, musky color of a lion complete with shaggy ruff and black muzzle. My body echoed my grandson's favorite expression—*whoa!* Every tendon in my hands and arms contracted, while my inner commentary exploded. *Our fences aren't high or strong enough. She'll get out; she is way too big to be around all my grandchildren; why do I listen to my foolish heart? She is strong—I won't be able to walk her without adding to my tendonitis? What is wrong with me? What was I thinking?*

This reaction is the polar opposite of the gentle tug of love experienced in the two weeks prior whenever I thought of Cobie. My hands grasped the leash tightly as I walked her from driveway to house. What was going on? Which was my truth: the belief that all would be well and trusting my intuition, or the fear and doubt embodied in my tight arms, hands, and shoulders?

A few weeks after Cobie's arrival, I met with my spiritual director. We always begin with prayer and silence. Occasionally she'll tell me what impressions she sees during our silence. When she didn't, I began sharing. About a half hour into our conversation, I mentioned the dog attack on my grandson, and she looked stunned, then shared what she saw in our beginning silence: me on all fours, cringing, looking up, terrified. She immediately connected this vision to the dog attack and how I felt then, but my heart knew the vision referred to my body's response to Cobie.

I prayed with this image, asking God, and my own heart and body, to help me understand. Despite the synchronicity of Cobie's photo appearing so randomly, the strong intuition to foster her, the constant reminders of her while I wrote about self-emptying, I reacted unconsciously upon meeting her from deep childhood beliefs. *The world is not safe. What I love will be taken from me. I am helpless to stop suffering. Following love is always wounding. I can't be vulnerable; I must be in control. I must be responsible; I must hold tight to everything. I can't let go or trust the unknown or fall fully into Love.*

While the mature adult in me truly believed what I told Cobie—don't fear, all will be well—at the same time, my inner child was crouching. That child was braced for loss or punishment, full of fear and mistrust in her intuition, her ability to communicate heart to heart. The cringing child expected others, society, or God to prove her foolish. My adult self then became aware I still feared loss, or more accurately, the inability to control my heart in loving Cobie so much already, and the eventual loss of giving her up for adoption. Somehow as an adult, I managed to blend an easygoing attitude with a desperate need for control.

Looking back now, I'm aware of three things. First, I'm sure Cobie felt shock and confusion that day being uprooted from her normal life, riding all day with strangers in strange cars, and being abruptly—albeit lovingly—deposited with me. My spiritual director's vision for me also seemed a perfect image of Cobie and her own fears and sensitive nature in entering a new strange world. Perhaps I felt some of what she felt. Second, the sight of Cobie automatically triggered a long-forgotten memory—that of my own sister being attacked by a neighbor's German Shepherd dog while I helplessly watched. My body remembered the past trauma, the horror I experienced over not being brave enough to intercept the dog. My body reacted in ways my mind couldn't comprehend. And third, as soon as I saw Cobie in real life, my inner knowing recognized an opportunity to heal, grow, and change. My heart just wanted to close down, saying a firm no to all this: to protect myself and put up guards, to take back my former wholehearted yes.

Somewhere deep within, I sensed taking this dog into my life was another symbolic surrendering, and like Don, I strongly dislike any disruption to the status quo, or the daily routines. Both my wholehearted yes to Cobie and the fear of what such a yes would require of me were my truths.

This self-awareness, this naming and softening toward healing helped me finally embrace Cobie with open hands and heart. I could release fear and give my tendons permission to relax. I could allow Cobie's story to unfold, trusting the healing love that brought her to me will bring her a loving "forever home." I don't need to know or tightly control the outcome. Whether she stays with us permanently or finds another family to love, I began to see Cobie as a channel for healing, an angel wearing a fur coat.

Just as Cobie's loving presence assisted in my healing, her gentleness with our toddler grandson, Jude, brought much healing to my whole family. I love seeing the two of them standing side by side looking out the back door, Jude's tiny arm draped over Cobie's golden shoulder. My eyes fill with tears when big dog and small boy stare into each other's eyes, nose to nose. Jude's dimpled hands cup both Cobie's cheeks as her big soulful eyes peer into his smaller ones. I'm moved by their tender presence with each other.

Self-emptying is the story of beauty and struggle. In the dog story, both Cobie and I sensed there would be upheavals. For the first two weeks with me, Cobie threw up every day. How oddly appropriate. Her daily regurgitation reminds me of my desire to constantly empty myself of old paradigms, old beliefs, and old traumas—all that is no longer needed. My journey becomes lighter, emptier, and freer as I align myself over and over with the Heart of Love.

Experiencing God: The Aroma of Letting Go

Sophia came to spiritual direction scattered and anxious. Settling into a chair she talked nonstop, words tumbling out until she looked up and noticed me poised on the edge of my chair, candle lighter in hand, listening, waiting for her to take a breath. My face must have registered the perplexity I felt over how to interrupt the chatter and help her center, because she grinned, then raised a hand over her mouth in an instinctive *oops*. She quieted, purposefully. Suddenly, out burst a little more, like a pressurized teakettle giving one last whistle as it's taken off the heat.

"I'm just a mess!" She moaned a litany of woes. "My shoulders are tight, my body hurts everywhere, I'm exhausted, I dread tomorrow, my mind is raging, and I can't be quiet."

She laughed at herself, sighed, leaned back, and motioned for me to go ahead. I sensed her body struggling to relax as I lit the candle signifying God with us.

She saw four bottles of essential oils sitting on my bookshelf: Frankincense, Peace, Clarity, and Release. She asked about them and I shared how I use them occasionally for myself and for others to enhance meditation and prayer. She was intrigued and asked to see the Peace oil bottle. Turning it over in her hand, she sighed again. I sensed longing in her sigh, so I asked if she would like to use the oils in our session. Her face turned as radiant as her *yes* was exuberant. I beamed back at her, hoping my smile expressed how delighted I was to be with her.

After explaining the method we'd use, she held out her hand eagerly. I gently poured a drop of Peace oil on her hand as she stated her prayer intention—*I desire to quiet my soul and center myself in God.* I invited her to rub the oil between the palms of her hands and inhale deeply. She rubbed her palms together, and then lifted her hands to her face, inhaling slowly. Continuing to breathe deeply, she sat with closed eyes, hands folded in prayer position in front of her face. Her body stilled as her shoulders dropped and her hands fell slowly into her lap. She rested them there on her knees, open-palmed. The silence felt amazingly effortless and holy. I closed my eyes too; the next moments were completely still as we meditated on being centered deep in the heart of God.

When I heard stirring, I opened my eyes and saw Sophia smelling the oil on her hands again. She was smiling with eyes closed. I invited her to remain silent as long as she wanted and when she was ready, she could simply begin sharing what she was experiencing. She sat silently for a few more minutes. When she spoke, her words came slowly, as if from a deep place. It reminded me of my son when he was little, how reverently he would pull out treasures from the depths of his trouser pockets to show me.

"I feel like a downy chick tucked under the wing of Momma hen."

"What is that like being all tucked in?"

"Like a trusting baby in the arms of God, peaceful, warm, and protected. I feel so loved." Her face glowed. Minutes passed; I looked at the candle flame, wanting to give her privacy and be prayerfully present to the presence of God. After a while, she continued.

"I feel one with the hen. I don't know if I'm really a chick under the wing or if I'm a feather on the wing. What part is me and what is God? It doesn't matter; I'm just centered in pure Love." I waited with her, savoring this love, this blessed silence. When she stirred again, I gently asked her to check in with her body.

"How are you in your body? What is happening with the tension you felt?

"Oh my," she said softly, a tear rolling down her cheek. "I'm so relaxed. My shoulders are down, not pulled up tight. My chest and belly feel open and light."

Later, she told me about something she called the backpack of her soul. She carried all her loved ones and all the suffering she felt for others in this pack. Intrigued and touched by this, I asked her to tell me more about it. What was in the backpack? What did it mean for her to carry it? Did it feel too heavy at times and was she carrying too much in it? She didn't know the answer to the questions and impulsively expressed the desire to be clearer about it. I reached for the essential oil called Clarity, opened the bottle, and held it out to her inviting her to take a whiff. She sniffed and instantly grimaced.

"Oh, that smells awful!" she exclaimed, then joked, "Maybe I don't really want clarity." We laughed together, and then discussed it for a moment, discerning what such a visceral response might be telling her. Again, I asked her to pay attention to her body—was this response triggering asthma or shallow breathing? Was it just a strong dislike for the scent? She closed her eyes and listened to her body's wisdom. "My breathing is normal. This is not triggering asthma symptoms. I may be afraid to be clear about the backpack, but even so, I want to continue."

I put a drop in her open hand and told her to rub her palms together but this time just rest her hands on her lap so the aroma could gently drift up to her face. She restated her desire to understand what was confusing about the backpack. We settled into silent prayer.

When she was ready to speak, Sophia told me her discoveries. She does carry too much in her pack and the weight compels her to do too much. She forgets she isn't God, tries to take over for God and does more than what she is called to do. And when she goes too far into the suffering of others, without being centered in God's heart herself, her soul is consumed with that suffering. I was moved by her honesty, but I sensed she was not finished, so I waited prayerfully in silence.

"There's more," she said aloud, tilting her head, as if listening. She closed her eyes and moved back into silence. After a few moments, I noticed her breathing deeply into her hands; her body shifted uncomfortably, and she abruptly opened her eyes. Conflicting emotions scurried across her features: perhaps confusion, fear, and shame. "I'm aware of an element of attention-seeking in my telling others I'm praying for them, putting them into the backpack of my soul. I'm proud of my ability to artfully say this. I'm also proud that I remember others' needs," she confessed. "It all makes me feel good, feel important. I remember reading about prayer; how prayer is sometimes more powerful when one holds another in prayer without having to tell them about it." She looked at me, openhearted and transparent, yet slightly horrified, shame evident on her face. I only saw her incredibly beautiful soul.

"Welcome to the human race," I said gently, smiling. She smiled back; we both knew this is the gem of insight hidden underneath all the layers of truth she gave voice to earlier. The process of deepening, of self-discovery and insight, of getting to know more about yourself and more about God can be exhausting and unsettling, so I invited her back into the arms of God. Once again we savored the feeling of being a little chick under the hen's sheltered wings.

After she again felt centered in God's love, we talked about how her self-expression was repressed most of her life. She mentioned the muted tones of her clothing, despite her love of color. I know her to be artistic, expressive, and dramatic, though she didn't allow this to show much. So, I suggested perhaps her flamboyant self needed an outlet, needed to be expressed, embraced, and integrated.

I told her I love the way she uses the eyes of her heart, her spiritual vision, to see how her genuine need for self-expression, if left unfulfilled or ignored, can manifest into a compulsion to gain attention by overly caring for others. Love attached to compulsion is not really free. Once she was able to accept and express her love of art and beauty, she would be freer to choose how to give attention to herself and to others in a more healing, self-aware way.

Our session was almost over when she mentioned her plans for the next day and the dread she still felt. She admitted her fatigue; yet, she had promised to be with her friend and couldn't cancel. She wondered what they would do, how she would make this a marvelous day for her friend. My own body suddenly felt tired, burdened by the weight of all her unspoken expectations of herself. I held out one more bottle of essential oil, called Release, and asked her if she wanted to try another scent.

"Absolutely. Yes!" She poured a drop on her own hand, handed the bottle back to me, and added, "I have no idea what I want to release though." I assured her it was enough to just be present to her desire. She quieted, and I sank deeply into prayer only to be startled by her excited voice. "I want to release control over tomorrow!" Bouncing to the edge of her chair, she continued, "Rather than try to make something happen, I am just going to think of tomorrow as two friends going out. I give up helping or controlling any outcomes."

"You will just be present to love?"

"Absolutely! Yes." She leaned back then, breathing a huge sigh of relief. It was so simple and so profound. We both wept. Then, we each grabbed a tissue from boxes near our chairs and laughed as we simultaneously handed it to the other. Our dear bodies reflected our thoughts, our beliefs, and emotions and how marvelous it feels—spiritually, emotionally, and physically—to ease into letting go, into trust. Our time was up. As she collected her things, I asked what it was like exploring prayer with all these different aromas.

"Wonderful," came her easy reply, face reflecting delight. "It's like being a kid again: playing, making new discoveries, and smelling God's perfume."

CHAPTER 9

Getting Over Ourselves

FROM INDIGNANT TO HUMBLE (SHARON)

Once, while I was at a friend's house, someone representing a local Christian church came to visit, offering to tidy up the kitchen. My friend Kay had just left an abusive relationship and her house reflected the chaos that was her life. After the woman left, I asked Kay what that was all about. Kay told me she met this woman at a knitting class and now she keeps showing up. She invites her to church and does things for her. Kay added she thinks the woman likes having a "project" to make her feel good. I was indignant.

"Doesn't it offend you when someone claims to be your friend but treats you as a project?"

"Kinda," Kay replied, grinning. "But, for now, the good Lord is sending me the help I need and I'm helping another feel good about her Christian self."

163

We laughed heartily. Humility can be fun! Kay and I both experienced humility in being gently asked to give up pride and receive love in the form it comes. I appreciate a gentle and funny invitation to not take my motives, or others', so seriously. Love is kind and lifts up the other. Love is not easily offended. Humility is in direct proportion to how well we love.

ॐ

He guides the humble in what is right and teaches
them his way. —Psalm 25:9

For all those who exalt themselves will be humbled,
and those who humble themselves will be exalted.
—Luke 14:11

Do nothing out of selfish ambition or vain conceit.
Rather, in humility value others above yourselves.
—Philippians 2:3

Finally, all of you, have unity of spirit, sympathy, love for
one another, a tender heart, and a humble mind.
—1 Peter 3:8 (NRSV)

All of you, clothe yourselves with humility toward
one another, because, "God opposes the proud
but shows favor to the humble." —1 Peter 5:5

TOO LITTLE HUMILITY (DON)

The most humble person I ever knew was a student from Bangladesh. For some reason, every move he made, everything he said, everything he did exuded humility. When he would approach you on the sidewalk, even though he didn't physically bow, it seemed like he did. Whenever he spoke, his words were carefully measured without a trace of egotism or self-importance. He listened more than he spoke. In his presence, I felt totally accepted, listened to, and cared for. He seemed to emulate Christ to me more than anyone I had known before—and he was Muslim. I asked a friend of mine who knew him well what this student did to make himself so humble. "It is not so much what he does," he said, "it is who he is." If anyone had a spacious heart, it was this student. To have a receptive heart requires a strong dose of humility.

For the most part, humility is not an admired quality in U.S. culture. A humble person is too often regarded as a wimp. Most people whom we admire—from politicians to athletes, musicians, and actors—are arrogant. Most of the people who "get ahead" in the United States do so at the expense of others, knocking them out of the way on their way to fame and stardom. Humility would seldom be used to describe their being or their behavior.

Christians don't seem to fare much better in our culture. This is despite the fact that humility is one of the most often mentioned characteristics of a true Christian in the Bible. There are some two hundred verses about humility, several of which I list at the beginning of this chapter. Unfortunately, the cultural characteristic of arrogance defines Christians in the United States much more than we care to admit or to imagine.

The guarantees of the U.S. constitution—individual rights, personal liberty, pursuit of happiness, and independence, so highly valued in our culture—tend to shape us more than the Bible. Unfortunately, this causes too many Christians to tilt much more toward arrogance than humility.

What Is Humility?

My computer dictionary defines humility as "a modest or low view of one's own importance." I like this definition. Having an exaggerated view of your own importance is arrogance. Having a modest view of your importance is a Christian trait: "Do not think of yourself more highly than you ought, but rather think of yourself with sober judgment" (Romans 12:3). Philippians 2:3 echoes this sentiment: "Do nothing out of selfish ambition or vain conceit. Rather, in humility value others above yourselves." When we "consider the heavens" (Psalm 8:3), we should have a modest view of our own importance. How can such a view be developed against the cultural current of arrogance?

Benedictine Humility

In the fifth century, St. Benedict of Nursia tried to teach his monks how to develop humility through a twelve-step plan outlined in chapter seven of The Rule of St. Benedict.[1] According to St. Benedict, this plan was designed to help them to achieve "a modest view of one's own importance." A humble monk:

1. Always has the fear of God before his eyes.
2. Loves God's will more than his own.
3. Subjects himself obediently to a superior.
4. Accepts distasteful duties with patience.
5. Confesses his failures completely.
6. Is content with little.
7. Believes and declares to others that he has no worth apart from God.
8. Does nothing that is not approved by the religious community.
9. Disciplines himself through silence.
10. Is restrained in demeanor.
11. Engages only in sober talk.
12. Is not only humble of heart, but lets others know that he is sinful.

This list does not resemble anything found in assertiveness training books, or in workshops, or in guides on how to get ahead or be a success. In fact, it seems totally out of sync with life as we know it. Yet the items on the list line up pretty closely with the Scriptures extolling the virtues of humility for Christians. Our culture, including too many Christians, has bought into assertiveness and self-promotion over humility, and we too often ignore the scriptural admonition, "in humility value others above yourselves."

I took the liberty of dividing Benedict's list into three categories: relationship with God, relationship with yourself, and relationship with others. Some of these categories overlap, but here's how I categorized each of Benedict's twelve points:

Relationship with God: (1) always has the fear of God before his eyes; (2) loves God's will more than his own; and (9) disciplines himself through silence.

Relationship with self: (6) is content with little; (10) is restrained in demeanor; and (11) engages only in sober talk.

Relationship with others: (3) subjects himself obediently to a superior; (4) accepts distasteful duties with patience; (5) confesses his failures completely; (7) believes and declares to others that he has no worth apart from God; (8) does nothing that is not approved by the religious community; and (12) is not only humble [mellow?] of heart, but lets others know that he is sinful.

Humility Is about Relationships

It is interesting to observe that half of Benedict's twelve points on humility have to do with relationships with others. Although a relationship with God and self is important, humility, the essence of Christian spirituality, is mostly worked out through our relationships with others. It is also interesting to observe that this book, which is about developing a more spacious heart, works mostly with a relationship between God and yourself. This is not necessarily bad, because we need to be centered on God and we need to become whole persons before we can relate well with others. Nevertheless, humility is most evidenced through a relationship with others, and Jesus agrees.

We return to Jesus' answer when asked about the greatest commandment: "'Love the Lord your God with all your heart and with all your soul and with all your mind.' This is the first and greatest commandment. And the second is like it: 'Love your neighbor as yourself.' All the Law and the Prophets hang on these two commandments" (Matthew 22:37-49). By this proclamation, Jesus shows the importance of the relational aspect of his kingdom. The Luke version (Luke 10:27) is followed by the parable of the good Samaritan.

There is no better illustration of the neighborliness to which Jesus was referring, but it is also an excellent example of humility. By lowering himself to serve someone who was considered a threat to him, the good Samaritan was showing humility. By providing hospitality to the victim whom everyone else rejected, he was showing humility. By placing the wounded man's needs above his own, he was showing humility. There is nothing in this story that affirms individual rights, assertiveness, or independence. In fact, it is a story of the interdependence of the human family. We need each other, not only to respond in compassion to each other's needs, but also to celebrate our joys with each other.

Jesus and Humility

Jesus provides us with the best example of humility. In chapter 2 of Philippians, we have the very well-known hymn of the early Christian church extolling the humility of Jesus, the same verses we used to show *Gelassenheit* in chapter 8. It begins in verse 5 with an admonition to all of us to be like Christ in his humility. "In your relationships with one another, have the same mindset as Christ Jesus." This mindset is one of self-emptying, self-abasement, humility, and a receptive heart:

> Who, being in very nature God,
> did not consider equality with God something to be used
> to his own advantage;
> rather, he made himself nothing

by taking the very nature of a servant,
being made in human likeness.
And being found in appearance as a man,
he *humbled* [my emphasis] himself
by becoming obedient to death—
even death on a cross!

This is the ultimate example of humility. Jesus left behind
the highest possible position in the cosmos in order to be hu-
miliated, mocked, scorned, and murdered brutally. There will
never be a better example of humility. As followers of Jesus,
we are supposed to emulate this self-giving, self-emptying,
and self-sacrificing humility. If you are like me, the humility
expressed in this passage seems a bit extreme, overwhelming.
We will never be that high and hope never to be that low.
How do normal people attain humility?

Footwashing As an Expression of Humility

Jesus left an example for "normal" people as well. In the
gospel of John chapter 13, he washes the feet of his disciples.
In an article for the church magazine *The Mennonite*, I wrote
about the humility shown by the act of footwashing:

> In Jesus' time, this act was part of showing hospitality
> to guests. Most of us know that servants or women were
> usually the ones who washed the feet of the guests when
> they arrived for a meal. A person of dignity, such as a
> teacher, a Rabbi or any man for that matter, would never
> lower himself to wash the filth off what was considered
> one of the most unclean parts of the body.[2]

In stooping to wash his disciples' feet, Jesus lowered himself from the higher position of rabbi, or the yet-to-be-under-
stood Messiah, to the inferior position of servant.

"Do you understand what I have done for you?" Jesus
asks in verse 12 of John 13. "I have set you an example that
you should do as I have done for you," he continues. This
posture of humility is what we must have in our relationships,

our interconnectedness, with each other. Pope Francis gave a wonderful example of such humility when he washed the feet of prisoners in Rome during a Maundy Thursday service soon after he was first installed in 2013. Can we perform such acts of humility in our daily lives? Can we humble our hearts to make them mellower?

"This stooping and bowing in humiliation and vulnerability in front of another person are not done easily in our culture," I wrote in the article on footwashing. "We no longer bow with our whole bodies and kneel to pray in our church services. We barely manage to bow our heads. Have we become too dignified to bow? To wash feet?"[3] I ask.

Are there ways that we can show humility in simple, symbolic actions? Are there ways to wash the feet of others in our daily lives?

Symbolic Acts of Humility

When my family and I returned from a three-year stint of missionary service in Mexico, I wanted to do something symbolic that would help remind me of my experience there, and I wanted to be reminded of my need to be more humble, to fulfill in a small way the verse from Luke 14:11: "For all those who exalt themselves will be humbled, and those who humble themselves will be exalted." I decided that on the campus where I worked, I would never enter a door before someone else.

For the most part this worked well; few people challenged my deference to them. That is until I encountered students from Japan. They were trained not to enter anywhere before a person of higher status; it was nearly impossible for them to obey my gesture to let them enter the door before me. This awkwardness was a further reminder to me of how much our relationships are defined by pecking orders of status, and how we unknowingly fall into these patterns without critical thought. It also helped me to lower myself, even if through a very simple act, to place myself in a more humble position than my status deserved within our cultural norms.

Jesus showed his devotion and his love to his disciples through stooping to wash their feet. By stooping, he made himself vulnerable; he made himself lower than others would have expected on the social scale and made himself humble. I was attempting to do the same thing by not entering a door before others, that is, to stoop, to show my humility. What stooping mechanisms have you developed to remind you of your need for humility?

Even though this should not be the goal of the humble, there is a positive side to vulnerability and bowing in servitude: "those who humble themselves will be exalted." This exultation might be an improvement in our relationships with other people. It might be a greater sense of God's presence in our lives by moving us out of our egocentric strivings. It might be a better understanding of our ourselves within the cosmos. Above all, it helps create a mellow heart. Whatever it is, like most spiritual truths, it's paradoxical. It doesn't happen by striving for it. In my experience, it mostly happens by accident.

According to our study, humility is mostly relational. "Clothe yourselves with humility toward one another," exhorts Peter in his first epistle. If we want to see how to clothe ourselves with humility, the best example we have is Jesus. He descended from the most exalted place in the cosmos to the lowest, bowing and stooping in humility. He also gave us a symbolic way of self-emptying and self-sacrifice through the practice of footwashing, one which we should practice. St. Benedict gave us a seemingly archaic but useful twelve-step program to humility, half of which is related to our interactions with others. It would do well for us to practice more of these steps no matter how out of step they are with current social standards. Following some of the examples in this chapter will go a long way to help us develop "a tender heart, and a humble mind."

᠊ᢞ᠊

EXPERIENCING GOD: HUMILITY, HUMOR, AND SELF-
. . . . EMPTYING (SHARON)

As I ponder Don's dictionary definition of humility, "a modest or low view of one's own importance," I glance sheepishly at a book displayed on my bookshelf, knowing I bought the book to make myself feel important. After a particularly grueling spiritual direction session with a well-educated person who had brought the book along to discuss with me, I keenly felt my own lack of college degrees and titles. My inadequacy compelled me to go immediately online and purchase the book. The book now enjoys prominent display, not because I love the cover or the writing. I never read one page. It is on display as a reminder that my importance is not measured by what I know or what I've accomplished. Humility is in direct proportion to how well I love.

There's a fine line between believing I'm important or knowledgeable enough to write about things that interest me and taking myself or my writing too seriously. Many people struggle to take themselves seriously enough. Self-diminishment is not true humility. Humility is not automatic through serving others or trying to be more relational. Service, rituals of service, and relating to others are vital and can indeed foster humility, but pride over our acts of service, our strong families, churches, or relationships is often there too, hidden in our unconscious comparisons. We can then serve from an "I-know-better-than-you" attitude.

I know this from my own experience. I've helped others through my high ideals and while firmly seated on top of a high horse. Perhaps this is why the movie (and book, although I've not read the book) *The Soloist* profoundly touched me. In this real-life story, columnist Steve Lopez desires to help a musically gifted homeless man suffering from mental illness. Steve discovers he is the one who is discontent with his life and learns more from the musician, Nathaniel Ayers, than Nathaniel could ever learn from him. Like Steve, I learned that sometimes friendship is all we can offer. Steve moved from wanting to help Nathaniel out of a sense of service or altruism, into humility and love, into allowing their friendship to change him as much or more than it changed the one he set out to help.

Though we often work and serve from mixed motives, it's good to become self-aware enough to at least notice when we serve or give with a hint of needing to feel important rather than out of love and with freedom and joy. True humility is best measured by how we love—by how willing we are to be honest and authentic in the presence of another. Pride and fear keeps us silent and masked. Humility shines when we are willing to get over ourselves, especially the importance of our opinions, likes, and dislikes.

As Don suggested, humility and self-emptying are closely related; one usually blends into the other. I define them both for myself like this: humility and self-emptying mean living with an open-hearted, undefended stance, aligning myself with love, not overly identifying with the inner commentary that goes on in my head, and not being strongly identified with my opinions, likes, and dislikes. I can have my preferences but they do not own me. All can be well with my soul; I can be happy and content with or without people exhibiting or life giving me what I prefer.

My favorite and most difficult personal experience of leaning into this definition happened when I was on a wisdom retreat. Heading off to this retreat, I felt excited, eager to experience retreat community and soak up all the wisdom teaching, but nervous over what difficulties I might encounter, too.

Three years earlier, I submitted my application for the retreat, answering many personal questions regarding my life journey, spiritual understandings, and physical health. The facility was not luxurious; only a few private rooms were available. Most students would share a room with another student or staff person randomly chosen. Each student would also work on the grounds or gardens in exchange for meals.

Three months before this weeklong school took place, I had unplanned surgery to remove my gall bladder and a section of my colon. I woke up from anesthesia with an unhappy colon and instant-onset irritable bowel syndrome. I was barely able to eat and, knowing the changes in my health might cancel my plans, I simultaneously prayed for healing while attempting to let go of my demands to be well enough to attend. I trusted God, ate as well as my digestive system would allow, and meditated in an attempt to calm my reactive colon.

Since private rooms were few, retreatants were notified that such would be granted to those in greatest need. Being an introvert, plus having physical issues that would need attention, I knew I would not get through the week without a private room. I needed the solitude and silence of a private room and private bathroom to recharge and relax my body enough to keep the colon spasms to a minimum. Unaccustomed to asking for what I needed, I hesitantly sent in my email request. The magnitude of my anticipation for this event and desire to grow in trust gave me courage. I was overjoyed when the event coordinator granted me a private room.

When the day of departure came, I was nervous and excited as I rode with Grace, another student. What would this week hold for us? Would I survive the food changes, the rigors of the retreat schedule? We talked excitedly during the whole trip; heavy downpours did not dampen our spirits. Pulling into the long lane leading to the dormitory, we wondered aloud what the instructor would be like in person. No other cars lined the gravel parking lot; we were the first to arrive. Having no idea where to go, we approached the first person we saw.

A small figure, back toward us and dwarfed in boots and winter coat topped with hooded rain slicker, was absorbed in the task of walking from one building to another. Expecting to meet the groundskeeper, we called out a greeting. A small face beamed at us, her cheeks ruddy and eyes joyfully peering out from under an enormous slicker hood. She introduced herself as the leader of the retreat, welcomed us, and pointed us to the building where we could register. I was enthralled by the quality of her presence, by her unassuming attitude. In that brief moment of greeting, she embodied the humor, love of life, and humility I imagine Jesus radiated.

We registered and found our rooms. Grace's room contained two single beds with a lampstand between them. I moved all the way to the end of the hall to find my room, opened the door, and rolled my small suitcase in behind me. My room included one single bed and lampstand with a window overlooking a lovely mandala-designed vegetable and herb garden. This gorgeous view seemed like a God smile, since I prayerfully create and color mandalas myself. I turned around to look for the bathroom and found none; my joy faded. I quickly went down to the registrant and discovered there were no private bathrooms in this facility. This wisdom retreat was originally planned for another location, but because of the increased numbers of retreatants, they moved it here. The information hadn't been updated. So, I had my private room, but the shared bathroom was all the way down the other end of the hall.

Here was my first difficulty. I went back to my room, sat on the bed, and breathed deeply, calming the panic hovering at the edge of my consciousness. I prayerfully expressed gratitude for this room and its location right above the main hall. I didn't have far to go if I needed to leave class and return to my room. I was grateful for the window over the mandala garden—the view would offer consolation and reminders to pray. I told God how thankful I was and expressed disappointment about the bathroom. Then, not knowing what else to do, I put a hand over my belly and blessed my colon.

Letting go of dwelling on my colon issues seemed the only thing in my control, so I promised myself and God I'd live in the moment and just allow my colon to respond to food and life however it would this week. I trusted the healing process would continue, as I stayed present to whatever arose, physically and spiritually. I felt whole in this tiny moment, not separated into segments of body, mind, emotion, and spirit. Not even separated into me and God, but whole—Being and being—experiencing what is right now. I was aware of the firm mattress below me, the emotions of anticipation and compassion, the inner stillness, the sights and smells of this place, my softening into trust, and my precious body with its layer of skin around all those sensations.

I unpacked and settled in, interrupted by only a few voices in the hallway as students trickled in. When I needed to use the facilities, I walked down the hall that emptied into the common room. The bathroom was on the left once in the common room. As I walked, I saw the door to the common room was open; ahead were comfy sofas and chairs gathered around a fireplace. Coming to the end of the hall, I rounded the corner and gasped, stopping quickly to avoid stepping on a figure lying prone on the floor. I stood there gaping at this person laying a few feet from the restroom entrance. When the spirit is confused, the cognitive takes over. My mind began labeling and questioning what I saw: a "legs up the wall" meditative yoga pose, someone deep in meditation. *Why would anyone meditate here, in this very public, bathroom-y place? It's unnerving!* As the intensity of my interior blustering dissipated, I tiptoed around the meditating person and made my way to the bathroom.

For some reason, I didn't recognize this incident as symbolic for my week. Or as containing what I've come to know as the way God's energy flows in my life. Usually, when I encounter surprise, humor, and unsettlement simultaneously, I'm aware God is offering me an invitation to play or grow in wisdom. This time, I was oblivious and shrugged off the meditating person's pose as the action of someone who was more extroverted or more comfortable with her body and her prayer than I was.

After that first flustered moment, my week flowed beautifully. Loving fellowship made being with myself and others effortless. I ate and slept well; nothing felt unsettling or overwhelming. The food agreed with me and the people were gentle and fully present. Our schedule was intense, but there was enough silence for contemplative, introverted folks to be comfortable. I soaked up all the teachings, the retreat's daily chanting, meditating, communal working, and eating. Every day's assignment involved paying attention to our likes and dislikes, but I had no dislikes. I was so grateful and prayed my thanks daily.

On Friday morning, the last day of the retreat, I was disappointed over not having any dislikes trigger me. I started to wonder if I was open enough, or if I was doing my inner work correctly. Every day, I observed other students lining up to talk to the retreat leader about their dislikes, their upsets, and their questions. I'd love a one-on-one with this dynamic teacher, but didn't wish to take precious time from those who really need to talk to her. A hint of jealousy arose in me, but ego tamped it down with quick consolation—*Perhaps I'm more advanced than the other students, so open and accepting that nothing bothers me.* I liked this thought, and believing I couldn't conjure up a dislike, question, or concern worthy to warrant getting in line with the others, I left the room after our morning session. I needed a break anyway and headed toward the restroom.

There was a stall in the women's room with no lock on the door. I had dodged the lockless stall all week. With only two stalls available for thirty-some women, that was almost a miracle. This time, the stall with a lock was occupied. Of course, break time was prime restroom usage and with a line quickly forming behind me, I reluctantly headed for the stall that didn't lock. I couldn't relax; I had to hold the door shut with one hand and keep my long sweater-coat off the floor with the other. Suddenly, a fiery ball of dislike exploded in me. All love and serenity evaporated. Jealousy, fear, and disappointment vied for dominance. I wallowed in insignificance, feeling unimportant. As I sat there, I was acutely aware of my body, my humanity, my spiritual nakedness, my vulnerabilities, and the paradox of wanting to be seen and fearing I'd be seen.

Love and intimacy are like that. We pull others close and want to be noticed, really known, but we push them away when they get too close to our hidden truths. True humility is best measured by how we give and receive love. Could I love myself enough to humbly embrace this dislike? Would I trust love enough to show God my spiritual pride and how closely connected it is with the pain of feeling invisible as a child? Could I trust the instructor enough to talk to her about this and my ongoing struggle to truly be at peace with my body and any meditative embodied prayer?

I'm glad this happened to me at the wisdom retreat. I was able to answer yes to all of the questions. I talked with the instructor and she gave me a delightful meditation that began a new phase of acceptance of my sensitive body, and while I never felt special that week, I felt loved and began to understand a deeper level of humility.

CHAPTER 10

When God Doesn't Show Up

TOY TRACTOR (DON)

My family moved off the farm when I was three years old.
Dad had to settle some affairs with the Ford tractor agency
where he had done business over the years, and he dragged
three of us children along in the car. Before he went in, he
explicitly warned us not to get out of the car. He would only
be there for a few minutes.

While waiting for him, I spied a toy tractor in the showroom window. I sneaked out of the car, into the agency,
crawled over a barrier into the window where the toy tractor was being displayed, and happily played with it. I don't
remember how I got back to the car before Dad, but my
other two siblings couldn't wait to squeal on me and my
disobedience.

We made the trip home in silence. I expected a scolding at best, and a whipping at worst. I suffered deeply awaiting my fate. Nothing happened. Several days later, my Dad surprised me with a gift of a toy tractor exactly like the one in the showroom window of the tractor dealership. I couldn't have been more elated. Instead of punishment, I received a reward. I received unmerited favor: the definition of mercy, grace, and forgiveness. Perhaps it was because I was only three years old. Perhaps he wanted to help me adjust to the recent move. Whatever his motive, I did not deserve what I received. Dad was being "merciful as God is merciful."

An understanding of mercy is necessary for developing a spacious heart.

ॐ

You, Lord, are forgiving and good, abounding in love to all who call to you. —PSALM 86:5

But God, who is rich in mercy, out of the great love with which he loved us. —EPHESIANS 2:4 NRSV

Be merciful just as your Father is merciful. —LUKE 6:36

Blessed are the merciful, for they will be shown mercy.
—MATTHEW 5:7

Joy at Someone Else's Misfortune

Schadenfreude. How I love to let that word roll off my tongue. It comes from the German and means "joy at someone else's adversity." We often revel in someone else's pain. Especially if we do not particularly like the person, or we think that such a person got some undue advantage, or is more successful than they merit from their performance. We prefer that they "get what they deserve."

Schadenfreude seems to be the natural tendency of most people in most cultures. *Schadenfreude* is the opposite of mercy. Mercy rejoices with people who get what they need, not what they deserve. Mercy is nearly as difficult to practice as humility because both of them require an abandoning of self and egotistical needs. To practice *Schadenfreude* and to withhold mercy helps to put us above other people. Reveling in someone else's pain in some twisted way makes us feel better about ourselves.

Mercy is also like humility in that it is done in relationship with other people; it is not a quality that one can find within. On the other hand, if we work on the spiritual practices outlined in other chapters, the likelihood is greater that our hearts will be prepared to show mercy when someone in need of our mercy comes to us. The person whose heart is prepared to show mercy is a person with an open, receptive heart.

Mercy involves a willingness to forgive. When Jesus was asked how often we are to forgive, his answer was a number meaning "an infinite number of times" (see Matthew 18:22: "seventy times seven"). In other words, forgiveness is required as often as forgiveness is needed. This statement is followed in Matthew 18:21-35 with the parable of the "unmerciful" servant. Many translations call it the parable of the "unforgiving" servant. That is because mercy and forgiveness go together. The real point of the story is the "merciful" or "forgiving" king. We are to forgive others like the king forgave his servant who had a huge debt. We are taught in the Lord's Prayer to "forgive us our trespasses [debts] as we forgive them that trespass against us [our debtors]." Forgiving is kingdom business. The person who can forgive has a tender heart.

Hearts of Stone

It is probably easier to find examples of people who do not show mercy than those who show mercy. I worked in a village in rural Mexico rebuilding homes that were destroyed

by a powerful earthquake. One of the families for whom we
built a home had used the title of their land to secure a loan
from a loan shark for a medical emergency. What had originally been a $1,000 loan, over the years had mushroomed
into a debt of nearly $10,000.

The man had no concept of interest or guaranteeing his
loan with the deed of his house. He needed the money immediately, and the going rate of 10 percent per week of com-
pound interest seemed, under such circumstances, a small
price to pay. The loan shark sent his lawyer to collect either
the money or the deed to his home and property. Of course
the man had no money and had to turn over the deed to the
only thing he owned.

I begged and pleaded with the man to show mercy on
this farmer, all to no avail. The more I begged, the harder the
lines around the lawyer's face formed. There was no mercy in
his heart, or in the heart of the loan shark he represented to
forgive this debt. I will never forget the sense of evil that per-
meated the room reflected in the face of the lawyer. "Blessed
are the merciful, for they will be shown mercy," states Jesus
in one of his beatitudes (Matthew 5:7). If this equation holds,
the people involved in crushing this poor man will not receive
mercy when they need it. Indeed, their hearts are stone: not
tender or receptive.

What I Need, or What I Deserve?

It is probably also easier to find examples of "justice" giving
people what they deserve rather than what they need. The
tendency in all cultures is to give out penalties and rewards
according to merit. As part of their social contract, societies
set up elaborate penal systems to punish offenders for the
crimes they have committed: the bigger the crime, the harsher
the punishment. This is not all bad. Without such systems in
place, anarchy would result. Nevertheless, some societies go
too far in trying to deter delinquents. In the United States,
the number of incarcerated persons continues to climb, while
evidence points to such incarceration often being ineffective

in deterring crime and worse at rehabilitating those eventually released from prison.

A new movement, which incorporates some elements of mercy, is called restorative justice. It focuses on the needs of both the victim and the offender, working at what each party needs rather than what they deserve, and in the process it restores community. It is gathering momentum in some areas because not only is it more effective in restoring relationships between the victim, the offender, and their community, but it also eliminates the need for building and maintaining the incredibly expensive prison system. God's mercy, giving everyone what they need instead of what they deserve, will probably never be applied to society in general, but if at least Christians would throw off their vindictiveness and operate with God's mercy, restorative justice might make more headway in our culture.

We all need mercy. The oldest words in Christian hymnody are *Kyrie eleison, Christe eleison.* In Greek they mean "Lord have mercy, Christ have mercy." The Jesus Prayer, prayed by millions across the centuries, also indicates our need for mercy. "Lord Jesus Christ, Son of God, have mercy on me, a sinner." We wrote about this prayer in earlier chapters. We all should be aware of our propensity to egocentrism, ethnocentrism, and socio-politico-religio-centrism. We can't help but push ourselves, our people, or our thinking to the fore, denouncing everyone or everything else that gets in the way. We also should be aware of our tendency to hide or project the seven deadly sins that reside in our unconscious: anger, lust, greed, sloth, envy, pride, and gluttony. If we are not aware of these sins and our need for mercy we are in denial.

Mercy: Unmerited Favor

Mercy is receiving or giving unmerited favor: undeserved compassion, unwarranted forgiveness. None of us deserves God's mercy or compassion. In spite of the punishment and death that we deserve for our propensity to sin, God offers us forgiveness and life. That is mercy—unmerited favor.

During a class in college a fellow student bragged about how he had slapped a paper together just a few hours before it was due the next day. In turn, I had slaved for several weeks on the topic, doing what I felt was careful research and thought. He received an A, and I only received a B. I was furious. In my mind, because of his track record and his generally poor study habits, he did not deserve an A.

Being merciful would entail rejoicing with my friend for his unmerited favor. Instead, I exhibited the typical human tendency. *Schadenfreude* is so much easier than mercy. Nevertheless, we are exhorted to "be merciful just as your Father is merciful." We are to forgive an infinite number of times, just like God forgives. Scholars have pointed out that the same saying is rendered in Matthew as "Be perfect, therefore, as your heavenly Father is perfect" (Matthew 5:48). Perfection in the kingdom of God is being merciful.

Story of Amish Mercy and Forgiveness

The Amish people showed a powerful story of forgiveness and mercy after the massacre of ten of their innocent children in a schoolhouse in Lancaster County, Pennsylvania, in 2006. According to our system of justice, the murderer deserved death—he did kill himself after killing the children. According to our societal values, the families of the victims were entitled to clamor for "justice" to right the wrongs that were visited upon them. If there were ever a case made for revenge, for hate, for vindictiveness, it would be now. Yet in a beautiful testimony of true Christian "perfection," the Amish chose God's mercy over the world's justice; they forgave the perpetrator.

Donald Kraybill, in his book *Amish Grace: How Forgiveness Transcended Tragedy*, interviewed the grandfather of the perpetrator's wife, Amy. "There's forgiveness in all this," he said. "There have been so many Amish stopping at Amy's house and expressing their forgiveness and condolences and bringing her gifts."[1] Kraybill claims that the hearts of the Amish, by their very way of life, had prepared them to forgive, and to forgive almost immediately. Their hearts were mellow. They were ready to forgive and show mercy because their "rhythm and rule" had prepared them. One of the objects of this book is to help us prepare our hearts with our own rhythm and rule. I will be discussing that concept in chapter 12.

The acts of mercy displayed by the Amish were not just visits and words of condolence. A committee was set up to give to the widow and children some of the $4.2 million dollars the Amish received from people around the world to express their sorrow at the tragedy. Not only that, but over half the people attending the perpetrator's funeral were Amish. The world was stunned—first by the tragedy, and then by unprecedented acts of mercy and forgiveness. The Amish went out of their way to extend mercy to the innocent widow of the perpetrator. Such an attitude is seldom seen in most societies, but it is a wonderful example of God's mercy.

Imagine the difference in feeling between those (most of us) who would harbor thoughts of revenge, anger, and resentment against the family of the murderer and the feelings of the Amish who offered mercy? Which heart would have more room for a spiritual awakening?

Mercy in the Story of the Prodigal Son

There is no more powerful story of human forgiveness and mercy than Jesus' parable of the prodigal son (Luke 15:11-32). After wishing his father dead by asking for his inheritance, then squandering it in rebellious living, the son decided it was better to return home as a servant than live in destitution. Instead of punishment or rebuke, the father forgave the wayward son and restored his place in the family. He even lavished unmerited gifts on him and threw a huge celebration for his return.

The son expected retribution. The son expected to work as a slave—what he deserved. He was willing to take whatever he deserved to atone for his sinful life. Instead he received unqualified forgiveness. He got God's mercy. "[God welcomes] his children home without asking any questions and without wanting anything from them in return,"[2] wrote Henri Nouwen. There are no conditions on God's forgiveness and mercy.

Beyond the unrestricted mercy that this story illustrates, God waits for us to come to our senses—to return home. Even though the purpose of this book is to see how we can prepare our hearts to be more mellow, more forgiving, more merciful, and more humble, these characteristics are not required for God's forgiveness. Likewise, we should not put conditions on others before we can extend our mercy or forgiveness to them. Being merciful as the father was merciful requires unconditional forgiveness.

Mercy Means Walking with People in Their Need

When I was working in an earthquake-ravaged rural village in Mexico, we received both material and monetary aid from many different people and organizations to help the rebuilding process. One such entity was a conservative Mennonite group of farmers from rural Chihuahua. They wanted to help, but they wanted to see the work we were doing before they gave their money. So we took them on a tour of our project. They didn't want to get out of the van to visit with people, or to hear their stories of loss. At the end of the tour, apparently satisfied with our integrity, they gave a very generous check to help us buy materials to continue to help more people.

Although we were extremely grateful for their contribution and their compassion (mercy) for their fellow Mexicans, we found it curious that they didn't want to become involved with the affected people. They were showing compassion to these needy people on one level, but denying their dignity on another. Their mercy was one-dimensional, even though I shouldn't judge what was behind their reluctance.

Many of our acts of compassion are done this way. We are content to put our money in the offering plate and not get involved with the people who are the recipients of our one-dimensional mercy. In my experience of working with marginalized and needy people, they would much prefer people offering them dignity by walking alongside them in their pain or loss than just receiving money.

A spacious heart allows us time to get to know people, whatever their social status or need. A receptive heart extends multidimensional mercy to everyone we meet, and especially to those who do not deserve it. In turn, our own dignity as children of God is restored.

We began this chapter by looking at our tendency toward *Schadenfreude* instead of mercy—with our rejoicing in someone else's misfortune. Rejoicing is a characteristic of mercy. It would be more like rejoicing in all things, except someone's pain. "Rejoice always," states 1 Thessalonians 5:16. "I will say it again: Rejoice!" we find in Philippians 4:4. Rejoicing is a characteristic of a mellow heart as well. We need to develop a rejoicing and mellow heart while offering mercy like God intended.

Joy comes from offering mercy and forgiveness where it is not expected and not deserved. This is a joy that celebrates when someone receives an undeserved reward instead of becoming resentful about it. This is a joy that my father must have felt when he gave me the toy tractor instead of more deserved punishment. This is a joy felt by the Amish who forgave their murderer. This is a joy that turns a heart of stone into a tender heart.

ೋ

EXPERIENCING GOD: KNOWING MERCY BY FORGIVING GOD (SHARON)

Forgive God? My title sounds a little blasphemous, especially if read with the mindset of theological absolutes. Besides the theme of this book being an invitation to soften our demands for absolutes, this particular section of the book is more about our experiences of God than theology. As Don stated, being merciful involves a willingness to forgive. We readily embrace God's willingness to forgive us, but are we equally willing to forgive God when God doesn't show up as we hoped? In a genuine relationship, both parties bring honesty and authenticity, even if the other is not understood; in any case, the giving and receiving is mutual.

A man I'll call Ben came to me for spiritual direction while on a weeklong retreat. He desperately needed peace and quiet, a respite from his chaotic world. Ben had been meditating on the story of Jesus calming the storm in the gospel of Mark. He wondered how the story would change if the disciples had been comforted by the sight of Jesus sleeping. Ben told me his life was like a boat tossed by wind. He was trying to keep his footing in the rocking boat, hollering at God to do something, but Jesus was just sleeping in the corner. I knew some of his life issues: a young daughter undergoing chemotherapy, an unfulfilling job, the death of his father.

I asked Ben what he felt looking at Jesus sleeping. He cursed angrily in reply, then quickly apologized. Sensing God was inviting Ben to be real in his prayer life, I told him it was okay to be angry. God wants our honest responses. Relationships are messy, including our relationship with God. If we never allow ourselves to be real in the presence of God, we are fakes. If we pretend we aren't angry, if we always show up in prayer as good and perfect, we silence our own voices and become caricatures of what we think Christians should be. We stifle any real communication.

I saw Ben two more times that weekend and was very touched by how tenderly God came to him through this passage of Scripture. During our first session, after his angry outburst, he told me stories of how helpless he felt as a young child, watching his parents' lives crumble. I listened and then invited him to imagine going into the boat with Jesus as a six-year-old boy.

When we met again, he described himself as a boy screaming at Jesus. I trusted what God was doing in him, so we stayed with this prayer of imagination, even as his anger increased. We stayed prayerfully present to the anger until he was able to just let it be there without needing to fix it, act on it, judge it, or be ashamed of it. As we stayed present, his body and mind quieted. He began to see hints of possibilities for his life that he couldn't see before.

In our last session, he again described himself as a child standing in the boat watching Jesus sleeping. Despite the yelling of the disciples, his childish gaze fixated on Jesus—his calm gentleness, his openness. Jesus did not need to control the storm to be at peace. We explored what this gaze evoked in him. After a long pause, he answered quietly: "I just want to curl up beside Jesus."

Ben left me that day a vision of peace and stillness. He knows when things get rough he can simply curl up with Jesus and he will be okay. Despite all the decisions and choices and storms of life, he can just curl up with Jesus and all will be well in his soul.

Before this prayer experience, Ben was unmerciful toward himself. He judged his anger as unchristian and repressed it, which only made him more frustrated. He thought he was angry with others and life circumstances, but he was really angry at his own powerlessness, his inability to change things. He was angry with a God who had power but wasn't using it. We are all like Ben. We get angry or depressed when we feel powerless, when God doesn't act when we think God should.

Barbara Brown Taylor writes:

> I want a safer world. I want a more competent God. Then I remember that God's power is not a controlling but a redeeming power—the power to raise the dead, including those who are destroying themselves—and the red blood of belief begins to return to my veins. I have faith. I lose faith. I find faith again, or faith finds me, but throughout it all I am grasped by the possibility that it is all true: I am in good hands; love girds the universe; God will have the last word.[3]

Writings like this help me move out of my own dramas and perceptions and help me forgive. Spiritual teachers help us move from our own smallness into the flow of love that has the last word and holds us in good hands.

It is almost impossible to accept or forgive our past—what was—or our present—what is—without first knowing the love that holds us in good hands. Without experiencing ourselves curled up in the boat with Jesus. The very act of moving closer to Jesus, of curling up beside him in the boat, means we are willing to find peace when we think there is none, and forgive God for not acting when we think God should be doing something. It means bringing our authentic selves to the God of mercy, along with all that we don't yet know or understand, so we can find comfort in both the calm and the storm.

Experiencing God: Knowing Mercy through Self-Forgiveness

When I was young, my family went to church every Sunday night. Only a serious illness kept us from attending. The evening programs were informal and often included Bible quizzes. I dreaded Bible quizzes. I am not a detail person and do not remember facts. Though I was very shy as a young child, I was also extremely observant. I knew some day I'd have to stand in front of the church to answer Bible questions. The thought gave me nightmares.

One Sunday morning, when I was nine, our pastor announced the next week's evening service would be a game of Bible baseball for all the children and youth. Filled with fear, I barely ate or slept that whole week. Nights were filled with desperate prayers: God, please give me the measles! Please God, make my dad get sick so we can stay home. God, cause a bad storm to blow the roof off the church!

It is traumatizing to be nine and powerless. I kept my fears secret. I was ashamed of my shy, inept self. Plus, in those days, shyness made adults think you needed more of what terrified you to help you grow out of it. Besides the horror of performing in front of anyone, I also hated baseball. I was not good at sports—mental or physical ones. In my active imagination I envisioned myself standing at home base, terrified of the thousands of eyes watching me swing and miss; those same faces were laughing at my wrong answers, fouls, or strikeouts.

The fateful evening arrives. I sit in the fourth pew from the front, awaiting my turn at bat. My stomach hurts; I need to go to the bathroom. Other nervous kids feel butterflies in their tummies, but in my belly, cannonballs hurtle about. I sit frozen, fearing punishment if I get up, fearing I'll vomit if I don't.

As batters score and give correct answers, the players move around the pulpit from one chair base to another, eventually coming back to the pews behind those still waiting their turn. My row slowly moves; we kids scoot along the polished benches toward the podium, which serves as the batter box. I'm a sweaty, sickly mess, dreading my time at bat, when fresh horror dawns on me. It doesn't matter whether I give a right or wrong answer this time, I'll have to go to bat more than once! I'll have to circle around this nightmare thousands of times before the evening is over.

The pressure is just too much. Right there in the second row, I do what no one dares to do in church. I cry. Out loud.

The youth leader a row behind me shuffles his feet. My crying continues; he leans forward and pats my shoulder. His touch does not make me braver. I desperately want some adult to tenderly excuse me from this nightmare, and instead I'm just patted like a baby. Like the baby I am.

Why doesn't the floor swallow me? I beg God to let me die, to make me faint at least, but God does absolutely nothing. I feel angry and abandoned, on top of feeling ashamed and terrified.

When it's my turn at bat, I stand as before a firing squad. I look at my shoes, too terrified to meet the eyes of the questioner. He shifts onto one leg, clears his throat, hesitates. I know he's thinking: *What should I do with this sniffling little mess of a girl?* I imagine his answer: *Use your kindest voice. And. Give. Her. A. Very. Simple. Question.*

"Where was Jesus born?"

This is a kindergarten question and I'm a third grader. The humiliation drains my brain. I stand in complete stupor; the silence in the church roars in my ears. My face is on fire. My eyes dart up and back down. The adults can't bear to watch; they are all closely examining their hands or their laps. Surely, they are praying: Dear God, please help this poor girl!

Just when I'm positive we'll all be frozen in place like this until the rapture, one tiny particle of my brain comes alive. An answer takes form and flies out of my mouth: "Nazareth!" *Whew, I said something!* I'm spent and so relieved.

I hear sighs skitter through the crowd. I'm suddenly appalled at my mistake but have no reserved energy to change my answer to Bethlehem. The questioner struggles between conscience and compassion. Then rationalizes aloud: "um . . . yes, um . . . Jesus grew up in Nazareth . . . so go ahead and take first base."

I move stiffly to the first base chair and sink down. I'm on full display with nowhere to hide. The small platform where I sit becomes my personal hall of shame. I fantasize running out of the building, knowing if I did, I'd probably get punished for disobedience. A kid gets a hit and I move to second base, but now I'm bawling and hiccupping in my attempt to hide my crying. By the time one of my classmates bats me home, I've sat for an eternity in utter humiliation.

When I am finally allowed to leave the platform, instead of returning to my seat to await another turn, I walk straight out the back door of the church. I find our old station wagon in the parking lot and climb into the back seat. I curl up there and wait for my dad to come punish me. I lay there crying, waiting for God to strike me dead with lightning. I wish God would hurry up, as I really want to be dead before my dad arrives.

An hour passes. I'm still in the car, alone with my vivid imagination. No one comes to punish me. No one comes to comfort me either. I wanted to be invisible in the church; out here it doesn't feel so good. My childish mind says I don't matter enough. No one cares about me, not even God. It is a long, lonely wait in the cold car without my coat. I image everyone laughing and eating cookies and brownies in the basement after church. I feel insignificant and angry.

When folks start spilling out of the church doors, I duck down out of sight. As the happy voices and footsteps retreat, the car sounds quiet; I risk sitting up. The parking lot is almost empty. I catch sight of Dad coming toward our station wagon holding something dark in his hand. I cringe, sure that Dad waited until everyone left; now he's coming to paddle me with a black hymnbook. I can't look. The car door opens. A dark green plate, full of cookies, is thrust in front of me. I glance up; Dad's expression is full of mercy.

"Here," he says. "You missed refreshments."

Later my family joins me in the car and we head home; not a word is ever said about the evening.

While I cherish my Dad's awkward tenderness that night, I lived with much unexpressed anger afterward. Eventually, I forgave myself for being so shy and sensitive, forgave the church for making me participate in Bible quizzes, forgave the adults for not helping me with my emotions, and forgave God for not saving me that night. It didn't happen overnight. Forgiveness takes time. Often it is an ongoing process.

Sometimes, as I prepare to offer something in front of others, the powerless, horrified nine-year-old shows up. And she won't allow my adult self to continue. I need to ask her permission to proceed. I give her the attention and tenderness she needs. I witness her emotions, her anger at God. I've even prayerfully imagined Jesus as a nine-year-old boy sitting on that bench beside me. When I begin to cry, he does too. Seeing his emotion mirror mine is incredibly healing. And I find mercy, forgiveness, and courage.

This experience infuses in me a strong desire to be a tender, merciful presence toward myself and others. When life is calm or stormy, when I'm joyful, angry, afraid, crying, or laughing, I want to find my way to Jesus and curl up next to love. More accurately, I want to know, deeply and experientially, that I am floating and swimming in a sea of Love—upheld, embraced, breathing love in and out, existing in love—always. Whether the sea is rough or smooth, it is impossible to remove myself from God's presence. Neither terror nor death, nor life nor joy removes me from this merciful, loving presence. And, as I learn to know this, to really know this, I want to open my heart and arms for all others to join me, to simply "see" love's embrace.

CHAPTER 11

A Laughing Jesus

JUST BE (SHARON)

My small grandson's favorite board book at my house is *Be Brown,*[1] by Barbara Bottner, the story of a little boy who gives his rambunctious pooch various commands. The little dog does not obey any of them. Frustrated, but willing to compromise, the boy shouts, "Be brown!" And the dog is brown. Pooch gets a "good dog!" and boy is happy. Jude always claps his hands in delight at the end. What a sweet example of not taking yourself and your rules so seriously.

This reminds me of a friend's comment to me as she dropped her children off at my house: "It's no wonder kids love coming to your place—you have no rules!" I wasn't sure if this was a pleasant proclamation, however exaggerated, or an insult. A world with fewer rules always appeals to me, no matter which side of the parent-child, leader-follower model

I'm on. Rules are necessary, but mostly we live by too many of them, especially the self-inflicted ones. I'd like to write a children's book that ends with "Just be!" so kids and parents alike remember how perfectly beautiful is it to just be alive for a few moments or hours with no pressure to do or serve or conform or accomplish anything. Just to live, to be awake and alive is enough.

ↄ▲

Truly I tell you, unless you change and become like little children, you will never enter the kingdom of heaven.
—Matthew 18:3

Remember the Sabbath day by keeping it holy.
—Exodus 20:18

A cheerful heart is good medicine, but a crushed spirit dries up the bones. —Proverbs 17:22

.... CHILDLIKE PLAY (DON)

Children live to play. In their play, they pretend to be whatever they want to be, using the time of play to discern what they want to be when they grow up. Much of their play is imitating the adults they see around them, but more of it is purely using their imagination.

As a child I wanted to be a professional baseball player. Everything I did revolved around playing baseball or softball with my friends. When there were no friends around I spent hours throwing stones at a telephone pole. A slab of stone on the lane served as the pitching rubber, and I was a world-famous pitcher who could strike out every batter and pitch a no-hitter whenever I was on the mound. Or I hit rubber balls with my baseball bat up against the barn. A grounder was a single, a liner of the wall of the barn was a double, and if I managed to hit one on the roof of the barn, it was a home run. I never made an out.

My play not only involved physical exertion, but also the use of my imagination. If I wasn't on my back staring into the wild blue yonder seeing clouds morphing into unendingly fascinating scenes, I was announcing imaginary baseball games while mowing the lawn. I was a king, a soldier, a missionary pilot, or a singer in a world-famous folk trio. I grew up without television, movies, and video games, so there was plenty of time to use my imagination.

Even though children today have many more distractions than I did, most of them still use their imaginations. I will never forget my daughter sitting in a corner either talking to herself, or talking to her boy doll, the ugliest doll on the shelf but the one she wanted. Sometimes the distractions of movies and television actually provide children with material for using their imaginations. Many students tell me their childhood fantasies involved playing the best known and loved characters from Disney movies.

Idle Hands Are the Devil's Workshop?

Somewhere between childhood and adulthood we are socialized to believe that play and use of the imagination are unproductive at best and evil at worst. My mother would often remind us that "idle hands are the devil's workshop." She meant doing anything that was not "productive" labor, so playing and using one's imagination were considered to be the devil's workshop. The Protestant work ethic has been so inculcated in our culture that most of us, whether religious or not, believe that play and use of the imagination are not the way to live or to survive in the "real" world. Combining this work ethic with the desire to accumulate both money and material things, U.S. Americans work long and hard. Most families need two incomes to keep up with their imagined needs. It is no wonder that burned-out, stressed-out workaholics are so prevalent in the United States.

Because of this, adults must learn to play in order to live. Supposedly our social system includes vacation time for us to relax. The average amount of paid vacation for most U.S.

workers is two weeks. In contrast, in most of Europe, the average amount is four weeks. The majority of U.S. Americans spend most of their vacation time attending family events, their two weeks parceled out in several three- or four-day allotments during holiday times.

In contrast, most Europeans divide their four weeks into two full weeks in the summer at the lake or beach and two full weeks in the winter at a ski resort. Or they spend their full four-week portion travelling to some exotic destination— for many that means visiting the United States or Australia. They would never think of spending less than that amount of time if travelling abroad. No ten-day ten-city whirlwind tour for them.

If U.S. Americans do spend time at a beach, or some other place of recreation, they take their work with them. Laptops, smartphones, a bag full of reports and analyses accompany them wherever they go. I remember sitting around a beach house with family members during a Thanksgiving family reunion. The adults, myself included, had either a laptop or a smartphone in our hands while we tried to have meaningful conversations. The children, and most teenaged and young adults, were all in their own worlds with their own laptops or smartphones keeping up with social media or games and texting their friends. We were mirroring our country's two inclinations for vacation: four days spent with family over a holiday, and taking our work along with us.

If that picture of our inability to relax and to "vacate" isn't dire enough, retailers have discovered another way to help us to "relax." Wherever there is a major tourist destination, whether the beach or serene Amish country in Lancaster County, Pennsylvania, hundreds of shopping malls and outlet stores have sprung up. Apparently we get bored being cooped up in a hotel room with our work and our technology, or the sea and nature can only hold our attention for so long, so we go shopping. We have to do something! "Idle hands . . ." I wonder if the "human doings" become the real "devil's workshop."

In contrast, when most Europeans go on their "summer holiday" to the beach, they leave their work at home. When they get to their hotel or campground, they sit. They cook and have long leisurely meals, often inviting others on holiday to join them. Often the same people return to the same resorts or campgrounds year after year. They converse and laugh together. They take a walk. They swim and they lay in the sun. They read a book and they sit. They sleep in and take naps. In short, they do nothing "productive." They relax.

They let their work-related problems and worries go. It's not that they don't know how to work. The Swiss and Germans that I have come to know actually work very hard. But they play hard, too. "When they work they really work," goes the German saying. "And when they celebrate, they really celebrate." This same philosophy applies to their vacation time as well. "When they relax, they really relax." I know this from personal experience, having spent several vacations with my Swiss in-laws at the beach. The first couple of days I was miserable because I kept thinking of what I could be doing. I wanted to check my email and see what I was missing. It took several days until I could finally relax.

Holy Play

Children live in order to play. Adults need to learn how to play in order to live. Perhaps this is why Jesus said that unless you become like little children you will never enter the kingdom of heaven. This can mean many things, but I truly believe it also means that we need to learn to play and use our imaginations. This is holy leisure: leisure that develops a spacious heart. A heart that is full of distractions of what to do next, worried about being "productive," is not such a heart.

In his book on leisure, Josef Pieper warns us about our inability to play. "In our bourgeois Western world total labor has vanquished leisure," he writes. "Unless we regain the art of silence and insight, the ability for nonactivity, unless we substitute true leisure for our hectic amusements, we will destroy our culture and ourselves."[2] Pieper contrasts "hectic amusements" with "the ability for nonactivity" much as I contrasted a typical U.S. American vacation with a European vacation. According to him, we need to learn "nonactivity" to be healthy. To sit, to rest, enjoy the "art of silence" and "insight." In other words, use our imagination. This is holy leisure.

Holy Hobbies

In our chapter on loneliness, I referred to having too much time on our hands as a cause of our restlessness and loneliness. If we use our extra time in soul-building activities instead of running after all the available distractions, we can mitigate that restlessness and loneliness. This extra time can be filled with activity as well as non-activity. Sometimes, as we shall see, the activity, when chosen properly, can actually put us in a soul-satisfying, nonactivity mode.

Hobbies can be such an activity and a form of play. Carl Jung, the famous Swiss psychiatrist, spent hours building a stone tower on a lakeside property he owned. This was one of the ways he got in touch with his soul. It was not work, it was a hobby and it was play—holy leisure. If I had to lay stone upon stone, it would be work for me.

Jung recommended some sort of similar activity for people who wanted to get in contact with their souls. Many people garden as play. There is something special about the connection to the earth that gardening provides: connection to nature, to the cosmos, and to the universal soul. Some find woodworking to be play, for others it is ham radio, working on cars, or model trains.

I once was a member of a club that bought an old two-seater aircraft which we refurbished until it was flyable. The time we spent working on the plane was pure joy. Watching the new plane emerge was like watching a butterfly emerge from a cocoon. This for us was like Jung building his castle tower.

Sports can also be a form of necessary play, both through participating and watching. However, because of the competitive nature of sports, I can get so involved emotion-ally that they are anything but relaxing. Some sports lend themselves better to holy leisure than others. I know from personal experience how a win or a loss can affect my mood, neither of which creates a mellow heart.

The point of these activities is not to be productive or to fill up time that we have on our hands. The point is to get in touch with our souls. When we are involved in an activity that we absolutely love, time seems to stand still. It is in these moments of suspended time that we are in touch with our souls. Some people have moments like this at their work. It would be wonderful if more of us could experience this at work, but too many of us are doomed to work that is drudgery. Therefore we need hobbies to help mitigate the day-to-day grind. Holy leisure in the form of hobbies can help us return to the creative God-image within us.

Holy Music and Reading

I do not know anyone who does not like some sort of music. I wrote about music in the chapter on cynicism, but I want to mention it in this chapter as well because of how playful music can be. The rhythm of music is in sync with our heartbeat, and as such it is in touch with the very core of life. To sing or to play brass and woodwind instruments requires using our breath, another essential part of our life. Music is often associated with movement, whether the gentle rocking of the parent singing lullabies to put a baby to sleep or the rapid-fire footwork of the flamenco dancer. This movement seems to be bred in the bone of most human beings and helps us connect with the universal heartbeat.

Retailers know how to lure customers with music, es-pecially during the Christmas shopping season. They begin playing carols in October to induce the shopper to think about spending. This is not my definition of playful, holy lei-sure; in fact, it makes me quite irritated. Yet I know many other people who are absolutely enthralled with hearing the "sounds of the season" once again, even in commercial settings. The holiday music does similar things to their souls as Mozart does for me.

Many people relax by reading. They pick up a book or ebook, sit on their back porch, easy chair, or bed to read. Reading, especially fiction, feeds the imagination and stills the soul. It helps us to relax because it takes us out of our everyday world and transports us into an imagined world. Any sort of reading can do this for us, because the mind is active while the body is relaxed. I have a friend who always has two books at his side. One is fiction and the other is some sort of devotional, spiritual, or self-help book. He reads one for enjoyment and the other for self-improvement.

Like music, there are all sorts of reading genres and preferences. What is relaxing for one person provokes the ire of others. I think a balance is important in both one's reading material and music.

Holy Laughter

Laughter is another activity of holy leisure that brings on a receptive heart. There is not much in the Bible about laughter and humor. In fact, there may be more admonitions against frivolity and humor than for it. In the rules for humility in chapter 9, St. Benedict admonishes his monks to "engage . . . only in sober talk." No telling jokes, no silliness, no fun! This was surely the attitude of many serious saints of the past; my grandmother was like this too. Fortunately, we have learned that laughter is good for the soul and for the heart.

When my wife, Esther, and I were working for a mission agency in Mexico and going through some very trying times, Esther's brother and family visited us from Switzerland over the Christmas holidays. He told us a story about their parents' visit to Esther and me in the United States just before we left for our assignment in Mexico. Esther's Dad got bored sitting around our apartment, so he spent many hours with a nearby farmer whom he had met at our church. In order to record the trip in pictures, he had borrowed a Kodak Instamatic camera from his brother that he could stuff in his pocket, without asking him how to use it properly.

When he returned home and had his pictures developed, he proudly gathered his family around him to show off his adventures. After showing the first three pictures, he wondered aloud, "Why is there an ear on all the pictures? Whose ear is that, anyway?" Apparently he was looking through the wrong end of the viewfinder when he was snapping pictures. All of his pictures were taken behind him, over his back.

Esther and I laughed so hard we cried. Later on when we retired for the night the story resurfaced and we laughed uncontrollably again. The whole bed shook with our guffaws. Because of some of the things we had been going through, we desperately needed that laugh. It helped quiet our souls. We retell that story whenever we need a good laugh, and it works every time.

"Laughter is the best medicine" is a much-repeated adage in English. It probably originated from Proverbs 17:22: "A cheerful heart is good medicine." This is not just folk wisdom, however. Science has proven that laughter is good medicine. According to his book, *Laughter: The Secret to Good Health*, S. P. Sharma writes, "laughter positively impacts various systems of the body. The benefits include reduction, control or prevention of high blood pressure, heart disease, peptic ulcers, depression, anxiety, insomnia, allergies and even cancer."[3]

Our overstressed society could use a large dose of laughter because nearly all the medical plagues of our time are in the list that Sharma presents. Our spirituality could also use a large dose of laughter. Laughter nurtures a merry heart and a merry heart is a mellow heart.

In this part of the chapter we have looked at the need for play in order to develop a healthy spirituality. We have defined such play as holy leisure and seen that both nonactivity and activity can help us to relax and develop a mellow heart. This includes using our imaginations, vacations, and hobbies, as well as reading, creating music, and laughing as forms of holy leisure. All of these activities can be used to develop a spacious heart and a healthier spirituality.

ॐ

EXPERIENCING GOD: ENCOUNTERING A GOD WHO LAUGHS
.... AND PLAYS (SHARON)

While walking the meadow with my dog and not-quite-two-year-old grandson, Jude, I stopped and got down on all fours to gaze at a spot in the grass. Jude soon came over and imitated my pose. I spread my hands wide until a patch of ground was framed between my thumbs and forefingers, making a square above the earth on which to focus our attention. I eased my body down flat in the soft grass, and then gently caressed a blade of grass with my finger. He flopped on his belly opposite me; our heads were almost touching. My fingers parted the grasses revealing a tiny crawling ant. His chubby finger swiped at the insect, but I gently took his hand and spread it palm down on the earth under mine, whispering reverently for him to just watch. Together we stared and silently marveled. He held this posture with me for a long time, just silently gazing at a square inch of ground.

This is the same child who comes to the meadow to blow off steam when his tiny apartment gets too confining. If a rambunctious toddler can learn to still his body and contemplate a tiny piece of creation, so can we busy adults. Most of Jude's and my time in the pasture is spent yelling and running around, kicking balls, or throwing toys for the dog. We roll and romp; in the evenings we sit on Adirondack chairs after lighting a mosquito candle and admire the sunset. I don't convince him to play and wonder; he just does. Again, we adults can follow the example of children and make time for play and wonder.

While Jude and I ran at the top of the knoll, Burren, our dog, bounded in the tall grasses at the bottom near the fence line. She was hunting mice and rabbits. Then, she too stopped to focus on the ground. Head cocked sideways, ears tilted toward earth and eyes concentrating on another small square of grass, she vibrated with the intensity of listening for the teeniest scurry or squeak. Then *pop!* into the air she leaped to pounce on whatever shimmied below. I hoped the mice and rabbits escaped her skills, yet I watched in wonder.

I love the wholeheartedness of dogs and children. They play, work, and learn with all their senses and their mind, heart, and soul. Their exuberance reminds me to choose a few things to do that I can be wholehearted about, rather than doing a lot of things half-heartedly or out of an egotistic need or obligation. Perhaps all children and dogs are old souls.

I experience God and connection to the earth when my senses are enlivened with playful wonder. Sometimes such oneness happens effortlessly; other times I consciously work at slowing down enough to really see things I normally overlook, and thus open my mind and heart to deeper experiences of earth and sky, of majesty and curiosity, of wonder and love.

Once, during my first year as a student at Kairos: School of Spiritual Formation, I was mulling over something that unsettled me during class. Mulling turned to brooding; brooding turned to complaining. I started blaming God for not showing up for me, for not giving me any consolations during the weekend, especially since all my classmates were sharing fabulous spiritual experiences.

I was sitting there pouting and harping when glimpses of red caught my attention. Running to the window, I saw two bright red cardinals hopping on the portico roof below the windowsill. I had a sixth sense for cardinals since they are my personal sign of God's love. Another cardinal joined the first pair. One bright bird with dark, round eyes under a scarlet, feathered crest hopped on the windowsill to observe me observing him. Hardly daring to breathe, I watched yet another cardinal land on the portico. Soon, there was a flock of cardinals scratching and skipping around the portico and flying from roof to tree outside my window. What was this? Do cardinals even move in flocks?

Suddenly, I experienced a deep sense of God laughing. Not mocking laughter, just the sheer merriment of lobbing cardinals past my grumpy self. If one can laugh a prayer, I prayed mostly heartily that day.

The experience of laughing with God is so precious for me that I naturally introduce the idea to others. A few times I've even displayed in my spiritual direction room a framed pencil sketch of Jesus laughing, his mouth open wide and his head thrown back in hilarious abandon. The first time I laid eyes on this image of Jesus, I knew *this* Jesus was the one that unconsciously carried me through my painful, too-serious childhood. My soul recognized this image of Jesus as the Love everyone talked about in reference to God. In a culture where criticism and judgment were fairly normal, where few were emotionally expressive and where affection was not naturally given, laughter and singing were love for me. I couldn't laugh at my imperfections yet, but observing laughter and laughing with others was balm to my soul. Since I was not comfortable with a hugging, affectionate God and repulsed by all the bleeding Jesus images, a laughing God was the perfect healing image for me.

Others who see the sketch of Jesus laughing are not always comforted. I'm somewhat surprised at times just how unsettling this drawing is for people. One woman asked me to put the sketch away; she didn't want to see it. She thought Jesus was making fun of her. Others react as if it's theologically repulsive to envision Jesus not being serious.

Many of us have grown up with somber images of Jesus, so a laughing Jesus feels frivolous or it mocks the seriousness of Jesus' life. How many of us grew up with solemn-faced images of Jesus: crucified Jesus, bleeding Jesus, passive Jesus, warrior Jesus, regal Jesus? Even the risen Christ is often depicted as restrained. From picture book to icons, we are spiritually formed by such images. We take Jesus very seriously, so it can be unsettling to see images of Jesus not taking himself so seriously. I hope we all become more aware of the feasting, laughing, and celebrating side of Jesus.

Two friends and I are in the beginning stages of planning day retreats for people to step out of the daily rush of life to rest, relax, and tend their souls. As we brainstorm ideas and toss the word *play* around, we notice our hesitation to use it in any of our promotions. If we include the word *play*, will people not take our retreats seriously enough? What is play to an adult? Will everyone assume play means art and games and shy away rather than welcome an opportunity to explore prayer, community, silence, or solitude in a light-hearted manner? We notice our own attraction and fear around the idea of using *play* as an invitation to relax and let go of some of the *shoulds* and *ought-tos* that sometimes bog us down.

I'll close this chapter with one more story. There are always laughable moments during holiday outings and sleepovers with our grandchildren. Children constantly teach me how to be completely present to each moment. It is Christmastime as I write this, the perfect season for me to slip into an idealized notion of love and glowing happiness that will surely happen during our planned activities. When my own children were youngsters, I often became discouraged and exasperated as hassles and upsets came just as often as the wondrous moments. Since then, I've learned to lower my expectations. I'm grateful for all the chances I get to show up differently for my grandchildren. Maturity and spiritual practices help me let go of idealism, embrace whatever happens, and engage life as it comes. It's freeing to interact with light-heartedness, to smile and remain openhearted through both the whining and wondering of children.

Over a recent Christmas, we took our three grandchildren to Landis Valley Farm Museum's night of Christmas carol singing around a giant bonfire. There was a live nativity scene at the church next door. I felt very excited waiting for the kids to arrive. Finally, they were bundled up and we were in the car heading out.

In that moment, while walking on the path to the stable with its softly glowing candle-lit luminaries, I said to my four-year-old granddaughter, "Rae, do you remember the story of Mary and Joseph and the baby Jesus?"

"Baby Jesus?"

"Yes, we're going to see a manger scene, with Baby Jesus and his family . . ."

Railynn interrupted, her words colored with awe. "We're going to *see God?*" Before I could answer, she turned to her smaller cousin, Jude, and said, "We're going *to see God!*"

We arrived and stood in front of the stable looking at the live nativity scene. Railynn didn't get it. She lamented of being cold and wanting to go home. I distracted her by pointing to the angel standing about three feet in front of us. "Look, Rae, an angel!" She didn't see any angel, so I put my hands on the sides of her head and turned her face in the angel's direction. "Right there, the man wearing white with a sparkly halo on his head."

She responded loudly, of course: "That's no angel. He doesn't have any wings!" After expecting to see God this must have been too great a letdown.

I couldn't keep from laughing. Not wanting to ruin the scene for others, I gently shepherded the children away. As we left, six-year-old Avery processed what she saw.

"I don't think baby Jesus wore a coat and sucked on a Nuk. But it was too cold for the pretend Jesus to be naked. He would have been cold and cried and that wouldn't have been good for a poor baby."

Since the biblical Jesus loved gathering little children around him, I'm sure he knew what their conversations were like. And I imagine him now, laughing boisterously with us over all this nativity confusion, his mouth open wide and head thrown back.

CHAPTER 12

Letting My Soul Catch Up with the Rest of Me

DRAWN TO THE SMELL OF FOOD (DON)

I was doing an errand in the downtown area of the city in Mexico where we lived. I was not a bit hungry. Nevertheless, on every street corner there were little booths selling a wide variety of foods: rotisserie chicken, taco stands with meats on a spit ready to be sliced for serving, and *chorritos*, the Mexican version of doughnuts. The aromas drew me to them. I entered the bank to complete my task, and upon leaving I was again accosted by the symphony of aromas. I couldn't help myself. I went to the taco stand and ordered some tacos in spite of myself.

I was looking to buy a home in a new city. When I entered one home, the aroma of freshly baked bread filled the air. I was immediately drawn to the house. Apparently realtors tell their clients to bake bread when they are showing their house because it draws buyers in rather than driving them away. What draws us to God and what drives us away?

શ

Finally, all of you, have unity of spirit, sympathy, love for one another, a tender heart, and a humble mind.

—1 PETER 3:8 NRSV

Draw near to God, and he will draw near to you. Cleanse your hands, you sinners, and purify your hearts, you double-minded. —JAMES 4:8 NRSV

Both Drawn and Driven

I am both drawn and driven in many areas of my life. I will illustrate this with my writing. I have been drawn to writing because it has been very cathartic for me. Writing has helped me articulate the many struggles I've had on my journey through life, especially when trying to integrate my cross-cultural experiences with my spirituality (see chapter 1). Writing has allowed me to examine the depths of my soul and doing so has helped me understand myself. I hope that by making my struggles public, I have been able to help others get in touch with their souls as well.

But my writing has also driven me. A good friend recently asked me if writing was addictive. Although he was careful not to make the question look like a direct comment on my behavior, the context made it clear that he thought I was addicted to writing. My incessant blog posts, my submitting manuscripts to various journals and my working on this book all prompted him to ask the question.

This assessment of what I considered to be important work caught me up short and made me examine my purposes for writing. I realized that I craved compliments on my work and if they were not forthcoming it drove me to think of new and more exciting things to write about, hoping to continue to see my name in publications and get the attention I needed. I decided to give up writing for a week. When I returned once again to put pen to paper, I had a new perspective. Yes, writing is addictive to me.

Indeed my writing drives me. Even though writing can be viewed as a "good" addiction, I need to have balance between being driven and being drawn. After all, an addiction of any sort is a sign of unhealthy behavior, no matter how productive it is. Addictions and obsessions are indications that we are driven, and are being controlled by our activity. Allowing ourselves to be driven by our obsessions indicates some sort of void in ourselves that we are trying to fill. My need for attention and continual positive feedback is the void I longed to have filled.

Driven by My Diet

Many years ago I was frightened by my high cholesterol and decided to do something about it. I found a diet and followed it religiously. My weight came off and my cholesterol plummeted. All that I had hoped for was realized in the diet, but I became obsessed with it. I couldn't participate in many delightful events because of what I could eat and what I couldn't. To make matters worse, I started to develop a "holier than thou" attitude toward those uninformed people who were ruining their bodies with what they put into them. I'm sure many people were annoyed by my sanctimoniousness, but I ignored them because I felt so superior. At first, this strict regimen changed my physical well-being for the better. But then it took me over. I became driven by it.

The diet was constantly on my mind, and I kept adding layers of severity to its regimen. With a dictatorial iron fist, I ruled over what graced our dinner table. I was obsessed. My diet, like my writing drivenness and many other obsessive behaviors, was probably an attempt to fill a void within my soul, a holy longing, that existential loneliness we discussed in chapter 7. Unfortunately, the void didn't go away with my strict diet. Like so many other addictions, it made the restlessness worse.

I no longer follow such a rigid diet, and although my weight and cholesterol have risen again, my soul health is much better. Because of the relationship between one's soul and one's body, I believe that my physical health is better as well. Since stress has proven to be a major factor in heart disease, the stress of my dietary strictness probably made me more susceptible to heart disease despite the lower cholesterol. My diet, like my writing, is another example of how even *good* disciplines can turn into driven, compulsive behavior. My heart had no room for awakening spirituality.

Obsessive Behavior and Addictions

Like my diet story, U.S. American culture is an obsessive-compulsive culture. We have stated this explicitly and implicitly throughout this book. It is precisely the reason we thought a book on a more tender and spacious heart was necessary.

We are driven because we have these little voices in our heads that tell us we are inadequate; that we should be "doing" something about our inadequateness. There was a little voice in my head telling me that I needed to lower my cholesterol. This voice kept getting louder and louder until it took over my consciousness. Did it take over my soul? I hope not completely, but the potential was certainly there. At such an extreme level, it is demon possession. Obsessive voices come from our socialization and whatever our childhood experiences lacked. They try to fill the voids that these inadequacies have left in us. My obsession was food. Other obsessions include drugs, sex, material acquisitions, endless distraction through entertainment, and even physical exercise and spiritual practices. We see these obsessions in our culture on a daily basis.

"Our addictions fill up the spaces within us,"[1] writes Gerald May, in his book *Addictions and Grace*. Through the creation story in the book of Genesis, May believes that God created us for love, and through the story of deliverance from Pharaoh in the book of Exodus, we were created for freedom. Because of our fragmentation (see chapter 7 on loneliness), we find it very difficult to fulfill our destiny as God's children and choose slavery over love. Slavery comes to us in the form of addictions. "The destructiveness of addiction lies in our *slavery* to these things, turning desire into compulsion, with ugly and loveless consequences for ourselves and our world," writes May. "The more we can understand about how enslavement happens to us, the more we may be able to turn in the direction of freedom and love."[2]

Our addictions drive us. My writing addiction drives me. My diet drove me. We are driven by our culture to be this, to do that, and to buy something or other. Like sheep we follow our culture's blaring call instead of the still small voice of God nudging us to draw near to him. We began each chapter of this book by describing a certain type of drivenness that is evident in our U.S. American culture. They are also listed below by chapter:

1. Driven to cynicism. Since so few things turn out the way we hope, we turn cynical.

2. Driven to hoarding and scarcity thinking. We amass huge quantities of material possessions and then defend these possessions with obsessive security systems, both on the personal and national levels.

3. Driven to obsess about the future or the past. We either obsess about our perceived unfair pasts or worry about our insecure future. Few of us are aware of the present and the great gift from God that it is.

4. Driven to resentment in the face of too many choices and instant gratification, among other things.

5. Driven to fear. Our motto "In God we trust" comes up short when we obsess about losing our security (especially since September 11, 2001), losing our cultural identity, and losing our privileged lifestyle.

6. Driven to either/or, exclusivist thinking. You are

either a missionary or a mission field. You are either
a liberal or a conservative. There is no middle ground
in this type of thinking.

7. Driven to loneliness. Modern life has driven us
away from community, nature, and integration of
our souls. We are fragmented and "double minded"
(James 4:8). The result is loneliness.

8. Driven to being in control. We are socialized to be
independent and to not to rely on anyone. When a
crisis hits, this supposed control that we think we
have collapses.

9. Driven to egotism and pretension. We are taught to
assert ourselves and run roughshod over anyone in
our way in order to push our own agenda.

10. Driven to vindictiveness and revenge. Justice means
giving people what they deserve rather than what
they need.

11. Driven to be productive. Fill up every moment with
some sort of activity so that we never have to reflect
on anything that might reveal our inner paucity.

The goal of this book has been to suggest ways to overcome our drivenness; to develop a heart that has room for
new expressions of spirituality. We hope that the suggested
activities will help us to be more drawn than driven. Drawn
to discover the God-likeness stamped into our souls. Drawn
to a closer relationship with God and mystery. Drawn to a
better understanding of others. Drawn to a spacious heart,
because according to James 4:8, when we draw near to God,
God draws near to us.

Being Drawn

In the opening story we saw how the aroma of freshly baked
bread and roasting meat draws people. I am also drawn to
music and to little children. Some people, like my sister, are
drawn to pets. Most people are drawn to stories. During a
sermon, when the pastor begins to tell a story, the audience

invariably perks up their ears. How can we live so that we are drawn in a similar way to God? Not driven out of a sense of duty, but drawn into God's presence because of the beautiful aroma emanating from God's being, God's love? The following story illustrates a place to start.

Drawn to Slowing Down

In July 2009, the Mennonite World Conference (MWC) was held in Asunción, Paraguay. Among those in attendance was an indigenous Guaraní man who had traveled from his remote village in the Chaco to Asunción, the capital of Paraguay, for the first time in his life. He came by bus, a nearly four-hour ride from his isolated village. Upon arrival, he was found sitting by himself in a corner. After nearly an hour had passed, a group of curious church leaders, wondering why this normally sociable man was so quiet, approached him to ask him if he needed anything. "No, I don't, thank you," he said. "It's just that the ride from my village to Asunción was so fast and furious that I am sitting here waiting for my soul to catch up with the rest of me."

Let my soul catch up with the rest of me. What sage advice for a driven culture. Allowing time for our spirituality to come into sync with the rest of our lives is the beginning point to becoming drawn. I spent most of my life driven to fill the voids in myself with newer and more exciting adventures, and changing jobs seven times and geographical locations eight times. My soul never had a chance to catch up with the rest of me. That is until I went inward as explained in chapter 1. By going inward, I recognized that my hyperactivity was making me more driven, more restless, more resentful, and emptier. Certainly not more mellow.

Drawn by Our Belovedness

Another way to be drawn to God is by recognizing our special relationship with the Almighty. Henri Nouwen, one of the most read and loved spiritual writers of our time, repeatedly told his audience, "You are beloved of God." If we remind ourselves of this fact over and over again, it begins to sink in that we are loved in the deepest place in our soul. We are made in God's image and likeness and are identified as children of God throughout the Bible. Understanding this relationship to God and the ensuing love fills the void that all our restless cravings and addictions cannot.

Whenever I lead a spiritual retreat, at some point I have the participants stand in two circles facing each other. I ask them to look into each other's eyes and repeat, "You are beloved of God." The experience is powerful. Because of the many wounds we have experienced in life, we need to hear this message over and over again. I tell people who come to me for spiritual direction to look in the mirror and repeat to themselves, "You are beloved of God." Again, for those of us who have done this, the experience is powerful. Those negative voices in our head that drive us can be replaced with these words of acceptance and love. These words draw us to God.

Drawn through Rhythm and Rule

Developing what spiritual directors call a "rhythm and rule" for one's life is another way to develop a sense of being drawn to God, of allowing our soul to catch up with the rest of us. Developing a rhythm and rule is paradoxical. On the one hand, we need to acquire a routine in our spiritual practices so that we can carve out space in our busy schedules to sit and let our souls catch up with the rest of us. The more often we sit in silence awaiting and sensing God's presence, the more often we are drawn to the awesomeness of that presence. This must be done regularly in order for us to be drawn like the aroma of freshly baked bread. The more we do it, the more our restless hearts are stilled.

On the other hand, we can become driven by our spiritual practices. Because they are done routinely they can become obsessive and take over our lives, much like the legalism discussed in chapter 6 does. Like with my diet, we can become slaves to our *holy* practices. As human beings it is impossible to have completely pure motives and intentions, but that should not stop us from trying to develop a routine that draws us to God.

Several years ago, as part of a sermon to my home congregation on "Resting in God's Presence," I outlined an ideal day of rhythm for myself that helped me to be drawn rather than driven. I share that with a few updates to make it current.

My alarm goes off at five o'clock in the morning. I prepare myself a cup of coffee. I spend forty to sixty minutes riding my stationary bicycle. During that time I reflect on any significant dream I may have had during the night, then I use my computer to check my email, to listen to a podcast of interest—either one with some spiritual theme or a funny one to exercise my holy laughter. I read a Scripture passage or some online devotional material.

At six o'clock, I go sit on my back patio for thirty to forty minutes no matter the weather. Sometimes I sit in silence, sometimes I repeat the Jesus Prayer over and over again in rhythm with my breathing, "Lord Jesus Christ, son of God, have mercy on me, a sinner." Sometimes instead of the Jesus Prayer, I repeat to myself, "I am beloved of God," or I use the Scripture verse I read, or the words to a song, using the spiritual discipline called *lectio divina*. Sometimes I think about what I had heard in the podcast or read online or reflect on things I want to write about. After my patio time, I go inside and sit still for fifteen minutes practicing centering prayer. I can literally feel the stress leave my body. I jot down some of my thoughts, feelings, and experiences in a journal from the patio session or the centering prayer time.

I am now ready for work. My day is usually filled from top to bottom with classes, course preparation, meetings, or student conferences. Running from one thing to the next can easily stress me out, so before going to a class, I pull out my class list. I go over the list, praying for each student. I do this before each of my classes. It changes my attitude as I walk into the classroom—both for the model and the problem students. I do the same before I walk into a meeting or have a student conference. My day has a much calmer feel to it, even though I have the same number of obligations as when I don't practice my rhythm and rule.

While I am eating lunch alone, I pray silently each time I lift the spoon or fork to my mouth. "Thank you God; you have given me so much more than I deserve." This keeps me from taking anything for granted and fills me with gratitude for what God has done for me.

After dinner, while I am cleaning up the dishes, I imagine each plate and each glass to represent someone whom I know in need of prayer—often my children and other family members or people at church or work. As I wash that dish or glass, I pray for that person. One can do this with any mundane, repetitive task. When I go to bed, I do a final inventory of the day, called the consciousness examen. I reflect back and ask myself, "Where have I experienced God today?" and "Where have I been so distracted that I blocked the presence of God?" Sometimes I discover God in the most unusual places. Sometimes a distraction comes to my awareness that needs to be dealt with, either in my relationship with God or with another person.

Generally, after a day with such rhythm and rule, I feel more grateful than resentful. My blood pressure is lower and I sleep better. I feel more drawn than driven. I wish I could say that every one of my days is a perfect reflection of what I presented. Some days I do all of the spiritual practices and some days I do none. Most days are somewhere in between with variations on the practices. Nevertheless, I have experienced enough soul rest from the days when I follow my rhythm and rule to be continually drawn to it.

When we are driven instead of drawn, it is difficult to sense God's presence in our lives. Our souls are still at the beginning of the bus ride waiting to catch up with the rest of us. We are double-minded and stressed, having divided loyalties. "Purify your hearts, you double-minded." We are fragmented. "No one can serve two masters. Either you will hate the one and love the other, or you will be devoted to the one and despise the other. You cannot serve both God and money" (Matthew 6:24).

On the other hand, when we are drawn, the sweet aroma of God's presence surrounds us like freshly baked bread. Our voids are filled, our compulsive behavior is quelled, our souls are at rest, and our hearts are mellow.

ớ▲

EXPERIENCING GOD: DRAWN TOWARD GREATER FREEDOM AND LOVE (SHARON)

My husband was quite exasperated with me in early December.

I confess to becoming adrenalized during the Christmas season. I was easily distracted and quite absentminded. It wasn't even due to lots of sugar and caffeine. My life was just full of exciting opportunities that had nothing to do with Christmas or shopping. Yet, excitement combined with the hype of advertising got me enormously revved. I'm not a shopper in any sense of the word. I avoid shopping, using everything way past its expiration date just to avoid going into a store.

My friend Brandi is the opposite. When in full creative shopping mode, she takes my breath away. This year, Brandi was on a budget; she shopped like a well-prepared, very skilled hunter going after an elusive buck. She was armed with store fliers, coupons, specials, door busters, and bargains. She assigned every person on her Christmas list an envelope. Across the center of the envelope was the person's name; on the right corner was written what Brandi wanted to purchase and on the left was the name of the store where said item could be purchased. Tucked inside the named envelopes were coupons, fliers, times of store openings, and anything else that might be helpful. Brandi planned her strategy after the Thanksgiving meal. Amid the gravy stains and dessert dishes smeared with pumpkin pie and grape jam, her table

was spread with fliers as she began the shopping prepara-
tions. Her eyes shone with the thrill of the hunt, joy of past
finds, and love for each recipient of each gift she was hunting down. Everything in the process was love, joy, thrill, and
skill.

My cell phone beeped with many of her finds the evening
of Thanksgiving and the day after: *Beep. "I got the scarf—
celebrate!" Beep. "Someone let me take the last doll on the
shelf—so grateful!"* She knew the Christmas season part-time
store help by name; they had bonded through many seasons
of Black Friday shopping. They rushed to assist her because
she was kind and joy-filled; they loved her spirit. Listening
to her and reading her texts I found myself getting more and
more buzzed. Like friends pumping each other full of rah-
rah-rah around the cabin fires after a successful deer hunt, or
before a football game. Adrenaline is contagious.

Then, the days following Black Friday brought an onslaught of emails proclaiming "lowest prices this year" and
"free upgrades with purchase" and "smashing sales." Even
normally quiet, small business owners began spitting pressuring, adrenaline-laden stuff into my inbox. If I don't take
time for quiet and solitude during busy times, and if I remain
adrenalized for too long, I become addicted to the rush. My
body and mind crank into overdrive. Once in overdrive, I'm
much less discerning, and more easily hooked and pressured.
So, washed in excitement, that year I overdid baking, holiday
expectations, and gift buying.

I entered December rather proud of my juggling ability,
keeping all my project balls in the air. I had always thought I
wasn't able to run a five-ring circus, but this season I proudly
moved between working on three writing projects, fostering
two rescued dachshunds and housetraining them, furnish-
ing a new office, buying gifts, decorating, and baking for
Christmas. *Adrenaline is your friend*, said my pumped-up
mind. I smugly agreed until empty ice cream bowls ended up
in the freezer instead of the dishwasher and my cell phone
and date book kept getting misplaced. Worst of all, I began

forgetting what gift I bought for whom and bought it again or ordered another gift online. I must have been a shop owner's dream with my forgetfulness.

I was disgusted. Not because I'd suddenly lost my scruples, or because I was watching myself turning materialistic. I was appalled I so easily switched from a contemplative stance toward life to a do-do-and-do-more stance. I'd succumbed to being driven by adrenaline and thrill seeking. Driven by truths other than my own. Jay's exasperation should have been my head's up, especially his displeasure at my buying frenzy. Shopping and gift giving are not my language of love; they do not expand my freedom or the quality of my loving. Keeping track of purchases and who wants what makes me absentminded, stressed, and pressured. This is the difference between being driven and being drawn. Brandi is drawn by her own heart to give and receive love through shopping and gifting. Brandi's love and freedom expands when she follows what draws her. I am driven by external pressure in an attempt to please people, thrill seek, or experience what Brandi is experiencing. My love and freedom is diminished when I'm driven.

This story obviously shows the difference between driven and drawn. In most people's experiences, listening to the still, small voice of God and the promptings of the heart grows subtler as one's skill in personal discernment matures.

I have another story that clearly illustrates the difference. As mentioned, I'm fostering two dachshunds. They are sisters who came from a commercial breeding kennel, and after two years in a contained, controlled environment, they do not know how to handle life in the real world. Both dogs, when frightened or curious, will lock into their kennel conditioning. They run back and forth from one spot to another as if they are still in their kennel run, back and forth, back and forth, almost putting themselves into a trance. It's neurotic but comforting to them. I blow a whistle, squeak a toy, or run opposite the track they pace to distract them. As soon as they look my way they get praise and a treat.

Conditioning and neurosis drive them into pacing. My presence, my call, and my treats draw them out of their trance toward freedom and love.

This is exactly the way of the human heart. The heart recognizes the Spirit's call to freedom and love, but the mind is comforted by its endless commentaries, conditionings, and neuroses. The heart is not right and the mind wrong; it is more the question of, do you want to be drawn or driven? Do you want to be controlled by your thoughts, conditionings, and addictions, or begin listening to the deeper drawings of Spirit? The heart always knows the difference—the way to be or the way to proceed. The heart can even discern between what's good, better, and best if my mind and body can be stilled and quiet enough to discern wisely. The best way to be or do always invites one toward greater freedom and love.

Experiencing God: Our God Images Form Us

Driven and *drawn* are my favorite words for describing personal discernment. For many of us, *discernment* is a heavy word. In my past church experience, it was only used for major decisions like choosing a new pastor, deacon, or elder, or prayerfully deciding what to do with property or monies for charity. Discernment was also used to describe the process of listening and determining if God is calling you to the mission field. Discernment was a group process; personal discernment for daily life was not taught.

The emergence of spiritual formation education in churches is changing this and many more people are learning to differentiate between all the voices clamoring for attention in their minds and souls. Personal discernment, deeper listening, is paramount to spiritual direction. In my experience of offering such direction, I find people really lack knowledge in this area and need companionship from me, and they need tools for practicing discernment in their lives. The Spiritual Exercises of St. Ignatius of Loyola are very helpful in learning personal discernment. One of the verses I use in guiding others through the Spiritual Exercises is: "I have set before you life and death, blessings and curses. Now choose life, so that you and your children may live" (Deuteronomy 30:19).

Whenever retreatants struggle with decisions, options, or ways of showing up in the world, I ask them which path seems most life giving. Which option expands both your freedom and your capacity to love? Freedom without a deepening of love might not be truly life giving. Which feels more draining, like death to your soul? Which path might be most life giving for those loved ones following your example of living after you have passed on?

Even as we ask ourselves such questions, we must understand how our images of God form us and impact our discernment processes. Our images of God are directly related to how we've experienced God in the past. If a God image is punishing, we will punish ourselves and expect life to be difficult and unsafe. And we will choose to serve or give beyond our capacity; this constant choosing what is difficult, year after year, begins to feel like the Christian path, the right path, and God's will for us. It is our image of a God with high expectations that drives us toward exhaustion—not our natural talents, our health, or energy levels. If our God images are comforting and move us toward greater wholeness, life will be comforting despite any difficulties, and we'll find it easier to balance self-care with loving and serving others.

A good example of the power of our stored images is how realtors know comfort sells houses. Most of us have images of a loved one baking cookies, the softness of a blanket when tucked in at night, swinging with other kids, candles welcoming us home. If a realtor brings her children along to swing on the swings outside a house, or lights a sugar cookie candle, or decks one bedroom with fine linen, the house sells faster. We are constantly tapping into our stored memories, conscious and unconscious ones, through smell, sight, sound, and touch. These memories are stored as images in our cells; amazingly, even as our cells divide, grow, mature, and die, our memories are passed on, cell to cell. Likewise, all of us have memories of God.

From a harsh parent to sweet-smelling incense at mass, from the magic of make-believe to a red bird sighting, from gentle baby Jesus in the manger to the way we grew up understanding the God of the Old Testament, from a big, warm hug to the grandeur of Utah's Canyonlands or the pollen-filled stamen of a lily, we have all experienced God. Our images of God, of Love, Goodness, Truth, and Beauty must grow with us, must heal and change, or our worldview and our very hearts remain stuck in the last images our cells have stored.

Countless folks, including myself, come to spiritual direction purposely to grow more intimate with the God of love: the receptive, intuitive, co-creative, unitive, relational Being, rather than only the God of patriarchy, of white men, of rational thinking, of rules and judgment they carry from their past. God energy is both masculine and feminine. Divine Love is both comfort and justice. Many have lopsided images and only certain kinds of experiences of God; many have God images that need healing.

One man could not look at the figure of a large hand cradling a small child that I have in my direction room. The inscription reads, "He holds you in the palm of his hand." The image and verse evoked a cruel God as it triggered memories of the large man who abused him as a child. One woman was very drawn to the figurine of a large, round Peruvian momma hugging a little child to her bosom. She often picked it up, held it in her hands and prayerfully gazed at it. Such gazing healed her too-harsh images of God. Another woman loved a wire sculpture made for me by my brother-in-law. In it a rock climber ascends a lava rock cliff while safely attached to harness and rope. For her, this translates into a God who climbs with us and keeps our souls and psyches safe.

As a very young child, I had a recurring nightmare. I dreamed a man with a hatchet came around the beds of sleeping children and chopped off whatever body part was sticking out of the covers. I resisted falling asleep. Much to the disgust of my older sister sleeping in the same bed, I pulled the covers up over my head, twisting them off her to keep them in place until I fell asleep. She told me many times she was not responsible for my suffocation. The man with the hatchet became my image of God, complete with the limited reasoning and immaturity of a five-year-old. I believed God would chop off any part of me that didn't toe the line, conform, be nice, or obey parents and elders. I also believed God would make me do horrible things for a living that I never had any desire or talent for doing—just because that's the way I thought God messes with people and tests their faith. After all, if God bloodied up his own son, why shouldn't he do worse to me? I grew up with this God image forming my worldview: life was not safe, life is difficult; suffering is required to be a Christian.

I became driven by this image—I must be perfect and sin not. And even then life was risky. Isn't my hatchet-man God image completely opposite the image of the Peruvian momma that hugs, forgives, and loves her child? Or the God that laughs in redbirds?

Like my story of Jesus showing me two yokes, one heavy and one light, we are free to choose our stance toward life, cursing or blessing, easy or difficult, energizing or draining, bound and driven or drawn by greater freedom and expansion of love. We are free to remain stuck and bound by our memories, especially our memories of God, or we can ask for new God images, be openhearted and receptive, and allow God to draw us in life-giving ways. Yes, we will have difficulties; the world is full of suffering, but God draws us in ways that help us live joyfully, in ways that are already part of our longings, our talents, our gifts to the world. And, whichever yoke we choose, the God who loves us more intimately than we dare believe will take up the yoke and pull along with us.

Epilogue

A mellow heart is one of the four "nonnegotiable essentials of Christian spirituality" as proposed by Ronald Rolheiser in his book *Holy Longing*. In our book we have called this heart an open or spacious heart, a receptive heart, a tender heart, as we have attempted to flesh out the meaning of a "mellow heart." In so doing, we have discovered that it is impossible to isolate one of Rolheiser's four essentials of Christian spirituality from the other three. In a way, a mellow heart is the glue that holds all four together.

The first of the nonnegotiable essentials is private prayer and morality. Throughout our book we mentioned times alone with God as important for developing a mellow heart. Perhaps the suggestions are different from the normal ways we think about prayer, but they are prayer indeed. We mentioned personal retreats, centering prayer, developing awareness of

God in mundane things, prayer of gratitude, holy breathing, the consciousness examen, and we even alluded in chapter 11 to "holy leisure" as being a form of prayer. Certainly the focus of prayer is to better our relationship with God, to learn to *know* God instead of simply believing in God.

The second nonnegotiable essential for a healthy spirituality, according to Rolheiser, is social justice. We do not make explicit statements on social justice but allude to it in several ways. The *unmellow* parts of our chapters on scarcity and abundance, gratitude, fear, cynicism, control, and mercy, all come as a result of the lack of social justice in our world. As we begin to work with our own personal brokenness and open our hearts more, we become aware of the brokenness of the rest of the world. This awareness should motivate us to reach out to heal others both as individuals and as members of broken social systems.

The third nonnegotiable essential for a healthy spirituality is participation in a community of faith. In spite of how we have been socialized, we are not disembodied souls sitting alone at a personal retreat soaking up the presence of God. We need to be in relationship with others, and we need to be in relationship with others who share our desire to fulfill the holy longings of our heart. Like beggars, we need to tell each other where to go to find food: food for the body and food for the soul.

In chapter 7 we wrote about the loss of community creating an existential loneliness and the need for us to covenant with God and with others in a community. In chapter 8 we wrote about surrendering to the providence of God and that the only way to do that is to allow ourselves to be dependent on others. For the Christian, that is best done within a community of faith.

A mellow heart allows us to bring together all of these essentials of a healthy spirituality. A mellow heart allows us to meet the demands of the other three without taking ourselves too seriously. Throughout the book we have examined many non-mellow elements in our culture. Our purpose has been to have us pause and reflect on what our culture does negatively to our spirituality and to propose solutions to these cultural propensities. We hope that our suggestions for developing a spacious heart, one with room for an awakening spirituality, will help you to develop a healthier spirituality, and as such to become a healthier member of your family, your community, and the world.

Glossary

Centering prayer: Centering prayer is a method of contemplative prayer that encourages interior silence. This prayer helps us let go of our thoughts and nudges us toward experiencing God's presence within us. It is both a relationship with God and a spiritual practice. Read more at http://www.centeringprayer.com/.

Consciousness examen: The consciousness examen is a prayerful reflection on the events of the day in order to detect God's presence and discern his direction for us. It is an ancient practice of the Christian church that can help us see God's hand at work in our whole experience. See more at http://www.ignatianspirituality.com/ignatian -prayer/the-examen/#sthash.OktFP6mw.dpuf.

Contemplative prayer (contemplation): The process of quietly thinking on God, our lives, etcetera, in a way that leads to action. Contemplation is key to spiritual formation and discipleship because without a quiet, undistracted focus on Scripture or our own lives in comparison to Jesus, we have a hard time seeing where God desires to bring transformation into our lives.

Guided imagery: Guided imagery is a gentle but powerful form of meditation that focuses and directs the imagination, often using words and music to enhance healing or bring a desired physical response (as a reduction in stress, anxiety, or pain).

Lectio divina: This is a way of prayer and reading Scripture that draws us into hearing from God and seeing the impact of the text on our everyday lives. It is a practice that should also be coupled with study of the Bible. We do *divine reading* by reading through a text slowly, out loud, and then spending some time quietly thinking on the words and phrases in the text.

Meditation: Meditation focuses our thinking on a passage of Scripture, or characteristic of God, or image of him in art or creation, or even a real-life event so as to see God more clearly. Meditation also helps us take apart the complex world in order to find a way to follow Jesus within it.

Total depravity: Total depravity is a religious concept developed especially by Calvinists based on the concept of original sin. Every person is born with a propensity to sin and do evil. This is to be counterbalanced by God's grace.

Endnotes

.... **INTRODUCTION**

1. Ronald Rolheiser, *The Holy Longing: The Search for a Christian Spirituality* (New York, NY: Image, 2009), pp. 43–70

2. Ibid., pp. 66–70.

.... **CHAPTER 1**

1. David Mazella, *The Making of Modern Cynicism* (Charlottesville: University of Virginia Press, 2007), p. 4.

2. Ibid., p. 4.

3. Ronald Rolheiser, *The Restless Heart: Finding Our Spiritual Home in Times of Loneliness* (New York, NY: Image, 2006), p. 54.

4. J. Philip Newell, *Listening for the Heartbeat of God: A Celtic Spirituality* (Mahwah, NJ: Paulist Press, 1997), p. 36.
5. Robert Johnson has written a good book on both dreams and active imagination titled *Inner Work: Using Dreams and Active Imagination for Personal Growth*. He writes from a Jungian perspective.
6. Newell, *Listening for the Heartbeat of God*, p. 46, quoting *Carmina Gadelica*, a collection of songs and poems of the Gaels.
7. Ibid., p. 46.
8. Don N. McCormick, *Companions: Christ-Centered Prayer* (Maitland, FL: Xulon Press, 2004), p. 109.

.... **CHAPTER 2**

1. Mary Jo Leddy, *Radical Gratitude* (Maryknoll, NY: Orbis Books, 2002).
2. Ibid., p.19.
3. Ibid., p. 21.
4. Walter Brueggemann, *Deep Memory Exuberant Hope* (Minneapolis, MN: Augsburg Fortress Publishers, 2000), p. 72.
5. Ibid., p. 71.
6. David Fouche, "Being Present to Toxic Culture: A Wake-up Call," *International Journal of Spiritual Direction*, Vol, 17, no. 1 (March 2011): p. 32.
7. Mary Jo Leddy, *Radical Gratitude* (Maryknoll, NY: Orbis Books, 2002), p. 27.
8. Henri J.M. Nouwen, *The Return of the Prodigal Son: A Story of Homecoming* (New York, NY: Random House Digital, Inc., 1994), p. 85.
9. Mary Jo Leddy, *Radical Gratitude* (Maryknoll, NY: Orbis Books, 2002), p. 7.
10. Donald R. Clymer, *Meditations on the Beatitudes: Lessons from the Margins* (Telford, PA: Cascadia Publishing House, 2011), p. 25.

.... **CHAPTER 3**

1. Henri J. M. Nouwen, *Gracias: A Latin American Journal* (Maryknoll, NY: Orbis Books, 1993), p. 123.
2. Ibid., p. 123.
3. Eckhart Tolle, *The Power of Now: A Guide to Spiritual Enlightenment*, 1st ed. (Novato, CA: New World Library, 2004).
4. Nancy Copeland-Payton, "Sacred Presence in the Losses of Our Lives," *Presence* 17, no. 3 (September 2011): 28–37.
5. Corrie ten Boom, *Clippings from My Notebook* (Marion, IN: Triangle, 1983).
6. Joseph Campbell, *The Portable Jung* (New York, NY: Viking, 1972).
7. Richard Rohr, *Richard's Daily Meditation: Contemplation in Action*, May 11, 2012. Sign up for these daily meditations at https://cac.org/.
8. Ibid.
9. Macrina Wiederkehr, *Seven Sacred Pauses* (Notre Dame, IN: Sorin Books, 2010), p. 77.
10. Ibid., p. 77.
11. Rose Mary Dougherty, *Discernment: A Path to Spiritual Awakening* (Mahwah, NJ: Paulist Press, 2009), p. 36.

.... **CHAPTER 4**

1. Barry Schwartz, *The Paradox of Choice: Why More Is Less* (New York, NY: Harper Perennial, 2005), p. 167.
2. Ibid., p. 104.
3. Ibid., p. 167.
4. Ibid., p. 167.
5. Mary Jo Leddy, *Radical Gratitude* (Maryknoll, NY: Orbis Books, 2002), p. 61.
6. "Student Credit and Debt Statistics," *Credit.com*, 2009, http://www.credit.com/press/statistics/student-credit-and-debt-statistics.html.

7. Brian Luke Seaward and Brian Seaward, *Managing Stress: A Creative Journal* (Sudbury, MA: Jones & Bartlett Learning, 2011), p. 46.
8. Mary Jo Leddy, *Radical Gratitude* (Maryknoll, NY: Orbis Books, 2002), p. 83.
9. Thomas Merton, *Thoughts in Solitude* (New York, NY: Macmillan, 1958), p. 33.
10. Wilkie Au, "The Practice of Gratitude," *Presence: An International Journal of Spiritual Direction* 17, no. 3 (September 2011): 10.
11. Cynthia Bourgeault, *The Wisdom Jesus: Transforming Heart and Mind—A New Perspective on Christ and His Message* (Boston, MA: Shambhala, 2008), p. 64.
12. J. Philip Newell, *A New Harmony: The Spirit, the Earth, and the Human Soul*, 1st ed. (San Francisco, CA: Jossey-Bass, 2011), p. 116.
13. Henri J. M. Nouwen, *Turn My Mourning Into Dancing* (Nashville, TN: Thomas Nelson Inc, 2004), p. 56.
14. Richard Rohr, *Richard's Daily Meditation: Contemplation in Action*, July 27, 2012.
15. Cynthia Bourgeault, *Centering Prayer and Inner Awakening* (Lanham, MD: Cowley Publications, 2004).

CHAPTER 5

1. Richard Rohr, *Falling Upward* (San Francisco, CA: Wiley, 2011), p. 6.
2. Barry Glassner, *The Culture of Fear: Why Americans Are Afraid of the Wrong Things* (New York: Basic Books, 1999), p. 48.
3. David Kinnaman and Aly Hawkins, *You Lost Me: Why Young Christians Are Leaving Church . . . and Rethinking Faith* (Grand Rapids, MI: Baker Books, 2011), pp. 96–97.

4. James Joyner, "U.S. Military Spending V. The Rest of the World," *Outside the Beltway*, April 11, 2011, http://www.outsidethebeltway .com/u-s-military-spending-v-the-rest-of-the-world/.
5. Scott Bader-Saye, *Following Jesus in a Culture of Fear* (Grand Rapids, MI: Brazos Press, 2007), p. 58.
6. Anthony de Mello, *Awareness: The Perils and Opportunities of Reality*, ed. by J. Francis Stroud (New York, NY: Image, 1992), p. 62.
7. Ibid., p. 62.

.... CHAPTER 6

1. Data from Harrisonburg City Pubic Schools website: http://www.harrisonburg.k12.va.us.
2. Charles E Smoot, paraphrased, *Fallen from Grace* (Maitland, FL: Xulon Press, 2003), p. 23.
3. Richard Rohr, *Falling Upward: A Spirituality for the Two Halves of Life*, 1st ed. (San Francisco, CA: Jossey-Bass, 2011), p. 13.
4. Henri J. M. Nouwen, *The Return of the Prodigal Son: A Story of Homecoming* (New York, NY: Random House Digital, Inc., 1994), p. 121.
5. Ibid., p. 113.
6. J. Philip Newell, *A New Harmony: The Spirit, the Earth, and the Human Soul*, 1st ed. (San Francisco, CA: Jossey-Bass, 2011), p. 117.
7. Quoted in Richard Rohr, *Falling Upward* (San Francisco, CA: Wiley 2011), p. 13.

.... CHAPTER 7

1. Ronald Rolheiser, *The Restless Heart: Finding Our Spiritual Home in Times of Loneliness* (New York, NY: Image, 2006), p. 9.
2. J. Philip Newell, *Christ of the Celts: The Healing of Creation*, 1st ed. (San Francisco, CA: Jossey-Bass, 2008), p. 50.

3. J. Philip Newell, *Listening for the Heartbeat of God: A Celtic Sprirtuality* (Mahwah, NJ: Paulist Press, 1997), p. 43.

CHAPTER 8

1. Donald Clymer, "Where Is Your Heart?" *The Mennonite* 15, no. 12 (December 2012): 20–22.
2. See http://www.gameo.org/ encyclopedia/contents/ G448.html.
3. Cynthia Bourgeault, *The Wisdom Jesus: Transforming Heart and Mind—A New Perspective on Christ and His Message* (Boston, MA: Shambhala, 2008), p. 64.
4. Ibid.

CHAPTER 9

1. Quoted in: Everett L. Worthington Jr., *Humility: The Quiet Virtue*, 1st ed. (West Conshohocken, PA: Templeton Press, 2007), pp. 52–53.
2. Don Clymer, "Do You Understand What I Have Done for You? Reflections on Foot Washing," *The Mennonite* 14, no. 4 (April 2011): 19–21.
3. Ibid.

CHAPTER 10

1. Donald B. Kraybill, Steven M. Nolt, and David L. Weaver-Zercher, *Amish Grace: How Forgiveness Transcended Tragedy* (Hoboken, NJ: John Wiley & Sons, 2010), p. 44.
2. Henri J. M. Nouwen, *The Return of the Prodigal Son: a Story of Homecoming* (New York, NY: Random House Digital, Inc., 1994), p. 22.
3. Barbara Brown Taylor, *The Preaching Life* (Lanham, MD: Cowley Publications, 1993), p. 11.